T0328773

Selected Essays on Economic Planning

MICHAŁ KALECKI

Selected Essays on Economic Planning

Edited, translated and introduced by
Jan Toporowski

CAMBRIDGE UNIVERSITY PRESS

Cambridge
London New York New Rochelle
Melbourne Sydney

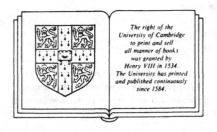

CAMBRIDGE UNIVERSITY PRESS
Cambridge, New York, Melbourne, Madrid, Cape Town, Singapore,
São Paulo, Delhi, Dubai, Tokyo, Mexico City

Cambridge University Press
The Edinburgh Building, Cambridge CB2 8RU, UK

Published in the United States of America by Cambridge University Press, New York

www.cambridge.org
Information on this title: www.cambridge.org/9780521179713

First published 1986
First paperback edition 2010

A catalogue record for this publication is available from the British Library

Library of Congress Cataloguing in Publication data.

Kalecki, Michal
Selected essays on economic planning.

Translated from Polish.
Includes index.
1. Economic policy–Collected works. I. Toporowski,
Jan. II. Title.
HD74.5.K35 1986 338.9 86-11790

ISBN 978-0-521-30837-3 Hardback
ISBN 978-0-521-17971-3 Paperback

Contents

Abbreviations

IMF	International Monetary Fund
OECD	Organisation for Economic Co-operation and Development
WOG	Wielkie Organizacja Gospodarcza (Large Economic Organisation)

1 Introduction by Jan Toporowski

Michał Kalecki is best known in the West for his pioneering work on business cycles in the capitalist economy. His originality and foresight in this branch of economics are now widely acknowledged. Less widely known, but nonetheless much appreciated by many of the *cognoscenti*, is his work on the theory of growth of the socialist economy, and the economics of the centrally planned economy. Furthermore, most development economists are aware of Kalecki's contribution to their field of interest. Perhaps least well known of all, outside Eastern Europe, is Kalecki's work on economic planning.

This is unfortunate for three reasons. First, it contains a fund of useful knowledge, of modest proportions but probably unrivalled quality, on the theory and practice of economic planning. This is of value to all those who are concerned with practical economic policy-making, since it contains illuminating insights into the workings of most existing economies.

Secondly, and perhaps more controversially, Kalecki's work on economic planning is central to the whole of his work on socialist economics, and his work on the theory of growth in a socialist economy in particular. This is a crucial as well as a critical assertion, since Kalecki's work on the theory of growth in a socialist economy has been used in isolation from his work on economic planning in order to support conclusions about the latter that are inconsistent, to say the least, with Kalecki's known views on economic planning.[1]

Indeed, it is possible to go further and argue that, outside the context of economic planning, Kalecki's theory of growth in a socialist economy is merely an interesting, but rather crude model. Its lack of sophistication is apparent in its perfunctory treatment of, for example, consumption. It seems, to this writer at least, that his theory of growth, although widely acclaimed in itself, only comes into its own and displays its true brilliance and originality in the way in which it expresses the essential dilemmas facing economic planners in a socialist economy, and analyses their resolution in terms of the information that is available to those planners. This is in contrast to most theories of economic planning that analyse planning in terms of information that is generally not available in practice. One suspects that Kalecki himself would have had little time for much of the abstracted model-building that absorbs many economists today.

Finally, Kalecki's work on economic planning deserves a wider audience quite simply for reasons of originality and intellectual precedence. Disequilibrium economics may or may not have died with the defection of Barro, but it is nevertheless interesting to see in Kalecki's writings on economic planning in the 1950s many of the most important tenets of disequilibrium economics that were enunciated in the West during the 1970s. It is striking that one of the seminal books that gave rise to this school of economists, Janos Kornai's *Anti-Equilibrium*, contains not one single reference to Kalecki in its 1971 edition. As with his intellectual precedence over Keynes, in his theory of the capitalist business cycle, Kalecki's originality has failed to obtain its just recognition through his 'failure' to publish more in English (or rather, perhaps, the failure of English-speaking economists, with some notable exceptions, to take much notice of developments outside the relatively closed world of Anglo-Saxon culture).

Any analysis of Kalecki's views on economic planning must start by placing them in their political context. Kalecki rarely wrote on politics *per se*. But in fact politics in its broadest meaning was never far from any of his economic analyses. Kalecki was a socialist with a profound concern for the welfare of ordinary people, from whose humble ranks he himself had risen. He despised the instrumental approach to economic planning, which sees the welfare of the masses as a means to the achievement of economic goals, whether the goal be the control of inflation, or the establishment of socialist plenty for future generations. Economic planning was to allow choices about social welfare to be made consciously, instead of haphazardly, as the outcomes of erratic market processes.

Kalecki started writing about economic planning during the early years of the Second World War. While working at the Oxford

University Institute of Statistics, he became associated with an organisation called the Socialist Clarity Group. This described itself as

> a small number of members of the Labour Party who work together with the specific object which is expressed in the name we have adopted. That is to say, we are attempting within the limits of our collective abilities to help in the work of clarifying Socialist thinking within the organised Labour Movement. All of us are individual members of the Labour Party, and most of us hold official position as Chairman, Secretary or E.C. Member. We include in our numbers a former Labour candidate, a production engineer, a N.C.L.C. Organiser, a railway worker, a University lecturer, a trained economist, a former factory inspector, a miner etc.[2]

The Group had a small publication committee, made up of A. Albu, B. Kelly, P. Gordon Walker, and W. N. Warbey. In the early years of the War they published a journal called *Labour Discussion Notes*. This campaigned for more energetic prosecution of the War against Fascism, and also carried articles on domestic policy. In the latter context, it promoted Kalecki's scheme for a more egalitarian system of rationing.

It is unlikely that Kalecki was ever a member of the Socialist Clarity Group, since he was not a member of the Labour Party. Indeed, he never became a member of any political party, deeming such membership to be incompatible with his independence as an economist. However, the Group asked him to give a lecture on the economic dilemmas that would face a post-War Labour government. The result was a paper entitled 'The Minimum Essentials of Democratic Planning', which was subsequently published in *Labour Discussion Notes*. In this paper he took a characteristically anti-Fabian approach. Some Labour intellectuals, he wrote,

> tend to think of planning in the abstract – they generally fail to distinguish clearly between different kinds of planning, serving different objectives, and they regard it as essentially a technical operation, to be achieved by intellectual persuasion and some kind of basic control, such as state direction of credit-creation and investment.[3]

In fact, he argued, there are fundamental differences between capitalist and socialist planning, with the former serving to strengthen capitalist social and economic autocracy. Nevertheless, socialist or democratic planning requires a strong state to articulate and promote the interests of the people against the pressures and power of monopoly capitalism – what he called capitalist 'power in society as a whole' and distinguished from the power of capitalists in their factories and their labour markets, which he called 'power over workers in industry'.

Kalecki later came to modify this view, in particular as a result of his experience of economic planning in Poland. There, capitalist 'power in society as a whole' had been fatally crippled by the War and the German occupation of Poland, when significant economic concerns were taken over by German companies or the occupation authorities. (Even before the War, German capital controlled a large and growing proportion of Polish industry.) Most of this fell into the hands of the new Polish government as the War came to an end. Subsequently, the private sector in industry was whittled down in successive campaigns to establish state control over the economy, and 'thrash out' capitalist influence in trade and industry. Employment in private industry fell from 134,100 in 1946, to 84,800 in 1949, while in the state and co-operative industrial sectors, it rose from 1.1 millions to 1.67 millions. Private wholesale and retail outlets fell by almost two-thirds and over two-fifths respectively between 1947 and 1949, despite the reconstruction of trade networks that took place at this time.[4]

In 1945, 1946, 1948 and 1950, Kalecki and his wife visited Poland, initially at the invitation of the Polish government, and in 1948 and 1950, when he was working for the United Nations, for holidays. On the first two occasions he was asked to advise on various problems relating to finance, rationing, and general economic issues. Until 1955, he stayed with the United Nations. In that year, he returned to Poland for good and took up the post of vice-chairman of the Planning Commission, just in time to play a leading role in the discussion of economic planning and policy reforms that was initiated in that year. It is worth noting that this debate was begun *before* the Twentieth Congress of the Soviet Communist Party, which is usually perceived as the watershed between Stalinism and reform. In any case, by that time the role of the private sector in the Polish economy, outside agriculture, was insignificant and the terms of the debate were completely different to those of the one to which he had contributed in 1942.

Again Kalecki took a characteristically clear, when not actually abrasive, line in this discussion. There were three broad strands of opinion within the discussion of economic planning reforms. At one extreme were the advocates of decentralised market socialism, in which the Law of Value, in the guise of market forces, would coordinate the operations of firms under workers' control. A less radical view was put forward by a band of reformers led by Wlodzimierz Brus. They advocated a 'guided market mechanism', in which central planning would be conducted by influencing the market environment in which the enterprises were to operate. Kalecki, however, firmly held to the view that central planning by parameters influencing the market environment had to be combined with the setting of quantitative targets and limits in an economy undergoing rapid structural change.[5]

In particular, Kalecki stressed the need to keep under the control of the central authorities the total wages fund in the economy, total investment and major investment projects, the prices and distribution of key commodities, and foreign trade. These he viewed as the most crucial variables whose control by the central planners was required in order to concentrate resources on development while keeping the labour and consumer markets and foreign trade in balance. Improvements in efficiency could be obtained, in his opinion, by using simpler and better incentives systems and rational organisation of enterprises and work. However, these could not be expected to make much of a difference in the short run, or at least not as much as was sometimes claimed for them.

Kalecki opposed the widespread use of market mechanisms outside the consumer and labour markets for a number of reasons. First of all, he argued that a profit motivation stimulating labour would need to be balanced by considerations of social justice and the special circumstances of individual industries and particular firms within a given industry. The allowances that would have to be made for these factors would blunt the effectiveness of profits as an incentive to work more and better.

Secondly, it was socially undesirable that workers should be made to compete by cutting costs, which would result in job losses and unemployment. In a striking anticipation of the 1970s disequilibrium theorists' analysis of duality, Kalecki pointed out that increasing efficiency by squeezing out surplus labour was not the same as providing this surplus labour with economically useful tasks to do and improving efficiency by increased production. Mere cost-cutting in a socialist welfare state would bring largely illusory improvements in the accounting performance of firms, since costs would be transferred from the firms' accounts to those of the state office responsible for paying unemployment benefits.

Finally, Kalecki pointed out that market mechanisms are indirect methods of transmitting information around the economy, in the course of which the information can be distorted or lead to distorted effects. Central control over the allocation of key products and materials was a much more effective means of executing the adjustments required by changing circumstances.

However, as recent experience has shown, democratic control over the organs of central planning is necessary to temper arbitrary decision-making and social irresponsibility. In 1956, as social criticism of Stalinist errors snowballed throughout Poland, it found an important mouthpiece in spontaneously organised and elected workers' councils that appeared in larger factories and places of work. Kalecki saw these as the organs of democratic control over planning. They were to act as a sounding-board for opinion on economic plans, govern the organisation of production in the enterprise, and safeguard opportunities for worker initiatives. However, they could not replace central planning and care needed to be taken to ensure that they would not wither away with the bureaucratisation of central planning.

Inevitably, the starting point for the Polish debate on economic planning in the mid-1950s was a critique of the then seemingly disastrous Great Leap Forward of the Six Year Plan of 1950–55. What had been, in its initial drafts, a comparatively modest development plan rapidly acquired the character of an affirmation of seemingly boundless faith in the socialist future and the creativity of the masses. By 1953, the whole project had gone appallingly awry. The exigencies of defence at the height of the Cold War in Europe (and the hot one in Korea); the construction requirements of the new factories and industrial plant that were to qualify Poland for the status of an industrial power; the peasant boycott of an increasingly strident collectivisation campaign; the escalation of total earnings beyond any possibility of satisfaction in the newly socialised retail sector; all these combined to discredit the Stalinist industrial strategy.

The lessons that were drawn from this experience were many and varied. At the time, the response of the dedicated activists who had promoted the Six Year Plan expressed the paranoia of fanatics caught in adversity: the difficulties were the work of counter-revolutionaries and saboteurs who must be exposed and eliminated.[6]

However, in 1956 the first secretary of the Polish United Workers' Party, Bolesław Bierut, died conveniently and somewhat appropriately while attending the Twentieth Congress of the Communist Party of the Soviet Union. He was eventually replaced by Władysław Gomułka. The latter had been under house arrest for his 'nationalist deviations', and he now replaced the discredited Stalinists with his own supporters.

The architect of the Six Year Plan, Hilary Minc, with whom Kalecki worked from the time of his return to Poland, was by now a sick as well as a politically weakened man and he retired in that year. The conditions were set for a more searching analysis of what had gone wrong.

No one denied that wrong decisions had been taken. But those seeking a more radical break with the practices of the past saw the cause of those wrong decisions in an over-centralised system of planning and economic administration that did not 'take into account the operation of the Law of Value'. In other words, harking back to the Austrian critique of socialist economics, the bureaucratic system of economic planning did not generate rational prices and would not allow a price mechanism to operate properly. Hence, having shut down the only correct sources of economic information, and deprived firms of the freedom to operate rationally, the system could not but fail to generate correct decisions. This has remained the conventional view in the West of Eastern European economics, and the basis of conventional wisdom on how the centrally planned economies can improve their performance.

Kalecki's view of what had gone wrong, rooted in his distrust of conventional 'equilibrium' economics, was different. In an article published in 1957 in the ruling Party's daily newspaper, *Trybuna Ludu*, Kalecki argued that it was more the content of the Six Year Plan, and especially its later, more ambitious, accretions that were to blame, rather than the system or, as it now became the vogue to call it, the 'model' of economic management. The plan had anticipated a very high level of investment which was not reduced as the defence burden increased. Too much of this investment was inefficient and directed to new projects, even where existing capacity could have been more cheaply adapted to the purpose. The assumptions about the expansion of agricultural production and foreign trade were hopelessly over-optimistic. 'These mistakes were not so much the consequences of the system of enterprise management as the cause of its extreme bureaucratisation and centralisation.'[7]

Thus the excessive central control that was the target of the 'Law of Value' critics was not at the heart of the matter. The economic problems experienced during the first half of the 1950s in Poland were started by an over-ambitious and inefficient investment plan, no part of which were the economic authorities willing to relinquish until it was too late. As the climax of the economic disaster approached, in 1953 and 1954, they were faced with seemingly uncompletable investment projects – uncompletable because there were too many of them relative to the resources available, and because too much of those resources had been diverted to the defence industries. In a desperate effort to lay their hands on the reserves that they hoped would enable them to finish those projects essential to the fulfilment of the Six Year Plan, the authorities centralised decision-making. Over-centralisation therefore was not a permanent condition of Stalinist economic management and development and the cause of its blunders, failures and inefficiencies. Rather, it was a desperate *tactic* adopted by the policy-makers in order to rescue what they could from the economic morass created by their own unrealistic policies.[8]

Despite his unwillingness to make the system, or 'model', of economic management the villain of the piece, Kalecki was far from seeing it as a 'black box' of policy-makers' exercises which have no effect, for better or for worse, on the economy. As is clear from the essays contained in this volume, he had plenty of suggestions for improving and reforming economic management. To those convinced of the unique efficacy of market processes, they may seem remarkably modest. 'Disequilibrium' economists and those with experience of working in applied economics, industry or planning, will find their originality, thoughtfulness and practicality stimulating and positive. But if in capitalist Britain Kalecki was a radical, in socialist Poland he was nothing if not a Fabian.

Nevertheless, despite this advocacy of gradual reform, Kalecki did not endear himself to the authorities for the outspokenness of his criticism of their policy blunders, and his support for working-class initiatives such as the workers' councils of 1956. He denounced the faith in the boundless possibilities of economic planning and the creativity of the masses, whose political activity was in any case discouraged. It was this optimism that repeatedly drove the economy into crises of over-investment, for which the masses paid heavily.

In the second half of the 1950s, Kalecki worked on a perspective plan for the economy covering the 15 years from 1961 to 1975.[9] In his draft, Kalecki proposed a conservative average annual growth rate of national income of 6.6% over the period. His reasons are well argued in his article 'On the Basic Principles of Long-term Planning'. Essentially these were that it is better to err on the side of caution and achieve a modicum of unanticipated success, than to err the other way, where even a small over-estimation of the possibilities will have much broader detrimental repercussions.

Kalecki's outline plan was widely praised as a highly original attempt at long-term planning. But his critics, inspired at least in part by a more sanguine desire to raise living standards, argued that greater efficiency in materials usage and increased supplies from the Soviet Union would enable that growth rate to be increased. Ironically, Kalecki was accused of failing to take into account the potential benefits from economic reforms. Optimism came in different forms at that time.[10]

Eventually, an un-Polish compromise was reached: the average growth rate for the economy was raised to 6.9%. In the first decade of the plan's currency, a disappointing growth rate of 5.7% was achieved. It was only after the addition of the first five years of Edward Gierek's import-led Great Leap Forward that the average annual growth rate of national output, over the currency of the whole perspective plan, rose to 7.3%.[11]

In 1961, the responsibility for work on perspective plans was taken out of Kalecki's hands and placed in those of the altogether less controversial Kazimierz Secomski. Kalecki continued work at the Higher School of Planning and Statistics in Warsaw, mainly on the problems of developing economies. But he continued to write on economic planning, as he continued also to write on growth in capitalist economies. For a while too, he remained a part-time adviser to the Planning Commission.

The key variable in all of Kalecki's post-War writings on economic planning is investment. It is this that determines whether the economy makes inadequate use of its resources, or is strained by pushing up against the barriers to growth created by the limits on the possible levels of consumption, imports and available domestic resources. In the short term, it largely determines the size of the economy's total wages fund, total employment in the economy, and future economic growth. Since the central task of economic planning is to keep the economy in internal and external balance while organising structural change, it can be inferred that the desired balance between the respective prerogatives of central authorities and enterprises will be approximately determined, other things being equal, by the proportion of investment in national income, or the investment rate.

A high investment rate, aiming to achieve rapid and wide-ranging structural change, will require a higher degree of central coordination of the economy. A lower investment rate would imply a relatively greater amount of routine decision-making, and would therefore allow for greater enterprise autonomy, with a lower degree of risk that enterprises' production intentions will turn out to be inconsistent with each other.

This last point is an inference which Kalecki nowhere, to my knowledge, makes explicit, except for references to the need for greater coordination of the economy when it is undergoing rapid development. Thus he states that 'the rejection of central planning . . . means either abandoning rapid economic growth, or dependence on permanent foreign assistance'.[12]

We may also add that rapid structural change not only increases the number of adjustments requiring central mediation and coordination, but is also more likely to distort the information on which market methods of information depend, as well as distorting responses to such information.

Central control over the investment process also plays an important part in avoiding what may be called 'decentralised investment cycles'. This is a phenomenon that, in theory, would occur in a centrally planned economy or a developing one, but is unlikely to arise in capitalist economies, which either tend to chronic under-investment (as in the United Kingdom), or have an accommodating financial system that ameliorates the effects of high rates of investment (as in Japan).

A decentralised investment cycle occurs when investment decision-making is delegated to enterprise management. Industrial management in developing economies is notoriously prone to seek to resolve its problems by additional investment. Janos Kornai calls this predisposition 'investment hunger', exaggerating perhaps the extent to which industrial managers are moved by what Joan Robinson described as 'animal spirits'.[13] As a result, when investment policy is devolved to them, an excessive number of investments is undertaken and the economy is propelled into a crisis of over-investment that can be every bit as acute as those of Stalinist times. Indeed, by comparison, it may last longer since its resolution usually requires administrative changes before decisions to defuse the crisis can be made effective. Thus central policy-makers (and their bankers in recent cases of developing economies) have to re-establish control over the investment programme, before they can thin out commitments and curb the enthusiasm of their industrial managers.

In post-War Poland, there have occurred two identifiable decentralised investment crises. One, a miniature one, took place in 1958–9. On this occasion, a reduction in administrative controls over decentralised investments led to the start of a large number of new projects. A fine spring and a dry summer in 1959 allowed work on these projects to be brought forward, causing serious bottlenecks in the construction industry and shortages of building materials. In July that year, the government was forced to intervene to reduce the numbers of existing projects and limit new ones. In September, ministries and local authorities were ordered to postpone a number of projects, and to reduce employment on the remaining construction sites to some realistic proportion of available materials. The result, effectively, was to recentralise investment.[14]

The other, and altogether more controversial decentralised investment cycle occurred during the 1970s. In December 1970, Władysław Gomułka retired from power after workers in the seaport of Gdansk had rioted and been shot down, while protesting at his policies of economic austerity. He was succeeded by Edward Gierek, who installed a new government of 'technocrats'. A key new policy was the reorganisation of industry into Large Economic Organisations (Wielkie Organizacje Gospodarcze, known for short as WOG – pronounced 'vog'), with powers to undertake their own investment programmes. Moreover, they were also given the right to borrow foreign currency if they could show that it could be paid back in future exports. What followed was the worst crisis of over-investment experienced in Poland since the War, combined with a foreign debt crisis which, while modest by Third World standards, promises to postpone any return to the relative prosperity of the mid-1970s until the 1990s.

Realising by 1975 that the whole strategy had got out of hand, the government attempted to regain control and re-direct investment. However, once an investment project is begun, it tends to slip out of the control of the central authorities and to come under the control of those directly involved in it. These are the firms for which it is being undertaken and the enterprises doing the construction work, both of whom have an interest in the survival of their project.[15] In 1976, the government drew up new investment priorities, and new regulations to limit the investment and importing activities of the WOG. But half-hearted efforts to set stricter investment criteria were no substitute for more direct methods. All that happened was that there were now additional investment projects, promulgated under the new set of priorities, competing for scarce resources. When, in 1981, the Western bankers would no longer lend, the crisis broke.[16]

Understanding these decentralised investment cycles is important for understanding Kalecki's views on central control over major investment projects and the overall proportions of investment activity. Not only do these cycles vindicate Kalecki's view, they also provide a dilemma for those who would place all investment within the discretion of industrial management to be determined by their assessment of the (socialist) market system around them. Clearly they would reply that 'investment hunger' could be kept under control by the 'hard budget constraint' over which Janos Kornai has agonised.[17] But one would have to ensure that this 'hard budget constraint' was not so hard in practice as to lead to chronic under-investment. At the same time, the long-term nature of many investment undertakings would require a stable financial environment. There is therefore no possibility of gradually approaching, in real time, 'optimally' hard budget constraints without throwing the investment process into chaos or simply discouraging such initiative. In any case, the 'hardness' of budget constraints would probably need to be differentiated according to the industry concerned. One can look at the experience of a successfully investing economy, such as Japan, and note that it has an 'accommodating' financial system, and that investment is controlled there by tacit government coordination in an economy dominated by cartels.

However, Kalecki by no means underestimated the difficulties involved in planning investments centrally, as the following essays show. Moreover he was certainly aware of the need for the highest integrity among central planners, as stories of his blunt criticism of them testify. But he knew that information that is only directly available centrally on the overall proportions of investment, the trade balance and so on, plays a vital part in ensuring that investment undertakings neither exceed nor waste available resources. It is this class of centrally available information whose very existence the Austrian critics of economic planning would deny.[18]

The essays that follow are written in the highly condensed and heavily streamlined fashion that is the hallmark of Kalecki's style as a writer. For this reason, it is useful here to outline some of the assumptions underlying Kalecki's approach, especially the ones that are tacit, or require further explanation.

First of all, with the exception of the first essay, these papers in the main refer to the economies of Eastern Europe in general and Poland in particular. At the time of writing all these economies were backward to some degree or other in terms of technology and infrastructure, in relation to the economies of Western Europe.[19] This is another reason why development plans and investment are at the centre of Kalecki's planning concerns. It is impossible to visit any of the countries of Eastern Europe and talk to its inhabitants without becoming aware of a widespread sense of backwardness in relation to North Western Europe and North America. Inevitably, economic planning is widely viewed as a means of realising the not-always-consistent aspirations arising out of that sense of backwardness (although this view is considerably less common now than previously, as a result of those planning blunders which Kalecki criticised). Kalecki refers to some of the difficulties that this may cause in his essay on the principles of long-term economic planning.

Would Kalecki's approach be applicable in a more industrially advanced economy? The conventional answer given by most economists is that it would not, or at least would need to be severely modified to allow for the different problems of 'intensive' growth that is held to be characteristic of industrially mature economies, as opposed to the problems of 'extensive' growth that is supposed to be a feature of more backward countries. Put simply, the latter involves bringing into production resources that lie idle because of industrial under-development. It is conceded that central planning, by organising the construction of modern infrastructure and new industries, can be more effective than reliance upon 'market forces'. But once the infrastructure is developed, new industries are established, and existing resources are fully utilised, then future growth can only be obtained by raising the productivity of those existing resources and production processes. The commonly held view is that central planning is inappropriate here and may positively hinder 'intensive' growth.

A more Kaleckian view, however, would be that it all depends on the degree of structural change that is required in the economy. If central planning is dispensed with altogether, then coordination of the economy rests with the financial system. This may be adequate to keep existing industrial operations up to scratch, if the government follows the appropriate monetary and fiscal polices. But following the appropriate policies consistently is a task that is by no means less complex than central industrial planning.

This still leaves the problem of long-term and structural industrial change. The assessment of this by financial systems in free market economies has proved itself notoriously ephemeral and incapable of sustaining a coherent industrail strategy in the longer term without recurrent financial crises, at least for wrongly backed industrial 'losers'. There is a sound case for arguing that certain innovations with repercussions for virtually the whole range of industrial activity, such as the micro-electronics revolution, require central planning for them to be effectively introduced with the minimum of financial and social dislocation. As long as there are benefits to be obtained from taking a broad overall view of the economy and modifying the activities of firms and industries in accordance with it, there will be a role for some degree of central planning in even the most mature industrial economy. That role will not necessarily diminish as maturity, however defined, is approached.

A second basic premise of Kalecki's in his approach to economic planning is the distinction that he made, virtually a decade before this was done independently by Janos Kornai, between the socialist economy as a 'supply-determined' economy, as opposed to the 'demand-determined' capitalist market economy.[20] In a socialist economy, it is the combination of social ownership of the means of production and economic planning that removes irrational financial constraints from production, which in a market economy are fixed ultimately by the state of effective demand. There is no doubt, in Kalecki's view, that in this respect socialism is superior to capitalism, since it allows fuller use of available resources, and does not make living standards dependent upon the vagaries of financial markets. Moreover, by making production less dependent on such financial markets (which ultimately determine the state of effective demand[21]), the socialist economy is more amenable to planning. This is because the productivity of investment does not vary over the period of the business cycle.

Hence, Kalecki saw economic planning as a crucial element in a socialist economy. Dispensing with economic planning, even if the means of production remain in some form of social ownership, would only make socialism more like capitalism and subject to destabilisation as effective demand fluctuates.

Obviously, this problem disappears if financial and market constraints at all times and in all places reflect real resource constraints. In the abstract world of neo-classical economics we know that they can be made to do so. The question for economists and economic policy-makers is: can financial constraints be made to reflect resource constraints reliably in the real world?

A second distinction that Kalecki makes is between the primary sector and the processing industries or manufacturing.[22] The two are distinguished by the fact that manufacturing uses as inputs the output of the primary (energy and extractive) industries. But they are also distinguished by the relatively greater capital-intensity of investments in the extractive and energy sector, and their long gestation periods.[23] It was his awareness of the different problems of investment in these two sectors that helped Kalecki to formulate his critique of the Stalinist doctrine of the need to expand more rapidly department I of the economy (producing means of production) as opposed to department II (producing means of consumption) in order to achieve self-sustaining growth. For, if productive capacity in manufacturing is expanded at a rate that is faster than that of energy and materials-saving innovation and the growth of primary industry's production, there will be shortages of raw materials and energy, and the new capacity will not produce at peak efficiency.[24]

On the other hand, the expansion of productive capacity in the primary sector is necessarily a slow and costly process in terms of the capital outlay required. Ultimately, the possible future rate of growth of a medium-sized and technologically backward economy is limited by, among other factors, the rate of materials and energy-saving innovation in industry, and the rate at which the energy-producing and extractive sector can be expanded, rather than by the rate of growth of the investment goods sector. Indeed, much of the debate around the economic growth projections in the first Polish perspective plan hinged on forecasts of Siberian mineral and energy resources and their possible rates of exploration and exploitation.[25]

Kalecki also uses this distinction in his criticism of what he saw as mechanistic incentives-based systems for inducing greater efficiency and productivity in industry. The manufacturing sector in Eastern Europe has traditionally been over-manned, in relation to the energy and raw materials available for processing (although not in relation to demand since, as we have seen, there is no 'effective demand' constraint). The way to overcome this is to expand supplies of raw materials and energy, and not to induce false economies by encouraging redundancies in manufacturing in the hope that surplus labour will eventually find its way into the primary sector. (It may in any case be unsuitable for this sector – e.g., in the case of women workers 'released' from an over-manned textiles industry – or the primary sector may require additional investment in order to create more places of work in it.)

Kalecki does not write much more here about the problems of inducing greater efficiency and productivity in the primary industries.

However, it is clear that he regarded calculated and well thought out programmes of investment as the key to this. We may add that the energy, extractive and primary process (such as steel-making) industries even on the most technologically advanced sites are still risky and dangerous places of work. Because of this, it is questionable whether increased productivity in these industries should be indiscriminately pursued. For example, the lengthening of the working week and weekend working in coal-mines, together with tacit encouragement of miners to ignore 'minor' safety regulations, became major grievances in the social backlash after the strenuous development efforts of the early 1950s and the 1970s.

Finally, there are the basic accounting assumptions that Kalecki makes about the distribution of output between consumption, investment and so on. Briefly, these are approximately the same as those used in the Material Product system of national accounting, as opposed to the System of National Accounts that, broadly speaking, prevails in the OECD countries. These are discussed in greater detail by Kalecki in his volume on the theory of growth in the socialist economy.[26]

Throughout these essays, Kalecki assumes no medium- or long-term borrowing from abroad to finance a temporary period of import-led growth. That Kalecki would allow only a limited useful role for foreign capital in socialist economic development is clear from his reference to 'dependence on permanent foreign assistance' (in the essay 'Workers' Councils and Central Planning'), and his essays on developing economies.[27] With Poland and some of the major developing economies embroiled in foreign debt crises of catastrophic proportions, Kalecki's caution was no doubt justified. But it is questionable whether there can be absolutely no positive role in economic development for a manageable modicum of medium- and even long-term credit, and whether borrowing from abroad should play no role in long-term plans.

Kalecki's attitude here was perhaps associated with his general reaction to a world monetary system and a trading dispensation that were dominated by the United States. He had personal experience of McCarthyism, and distrusted American trading and lending policies almost as much as he loathed American foreign policy. For him these were summed up in the sordid economics and politics of Latin America in the 1950s, and the murderous war in Vietnam in the 1960s.

At the time when he was writing, developing countries could only borrow officially for the short term (other than trade credits) from the International Monetary Fund and, for longer term development projects, from the International Bank for Reconstruction and Development (the World Bank). Poland itself was a member of the IMF until 1950. The United States has the greatest say in the policies of these institutions, perhaps even more so in Kalecki's day than now. Their use by the US as virtual instruments of American foreign and trading policy made Kalecki understandably suspicious of borrowing from them. The alternative of borrowing in the commercial and less overtly politically interested Eurocurrency markets, the opium of economic planners and policy-makers in the 1970s, did not really develop on any significant scale until the second half of the 1960s. It was this alternative that proved politically palatable and ultimately irresistible to the Polish government in the 1970s.

More strikingly unrealistic is Kalecki's rather easy assertion that, in a socialist economy, the central policy-makers can conduct a flexible pricing policy to avoid undesirable fluctuations in effective demand, and that this is one of the advantages of socialism over capitalism.[28] After recurrent 'meat crises' and two decades in which the Polish authorities have been pinioned by social unrest to patently unrealistic food prices, it is surely impossible to hold to the view that pricing policy can be conducted at the discretion of the central economic policy-makers. This could only occur under a system of total economic autocracy, which Kalecki made clear was repugnant to him, or in a system of socialist democracy in which a consensus on distributional matters, informed by expert opinion, could emerge. Significantly, the Hungarian experience in respect of pricing policy has been different to that of Poland.

This brings us to another gap in these essays. While Kalecki had a well-developed conception about industrial organisation and the role of workers' councils in securing socialist democracy *at the point of production*, a crucial lacuna remains in his theory concerning the determination of central plans *after* workers' councils have added their comments and suggestions. At the time when Kalecki was writing, annual and five year plans in Poland were approved in their final form by the Polish parliament, the Sejm. However, in most years this has been a mere rubber-stamping formality, preceded by little substantial amendment in the Sejm, and often followed by considerable and arbitrary alteration. There is no doubt that Kalecki envisaged some process whereby a social agreement is arrived at, after advice from economists, engineers and planners on the growth, consumption and investment alternatives facing the economy. But the organisation of the political process of policy-making remains, in his work, incomplete.

Finally, in his 'Principles of Long-term Planning', Kalecki seems to presume that short-term foreign trade credits are virtually unavailable. While this may have been a problem for Poland at the time when Kalecki was writing, there is no reason now why even a socialist country should not have access to such credits, as long as it is not in difficulties with its foreign trade or debts.

In translating these essays, I have tried to keep as close to Kalecki's original account as possible. In the case of the first essay on 'The Essentials for Democratic Planning', which Kalecki wrote in English, I have reproduced the original with only minor alterations, made after reference to Kalecki's Polish translation, which is contained in the third volume of his Collected works. The first half of the essay on 'Problems in the Theory of Growth of a Socialist Economy', an early version of his *An Introduction to the Theory of Growth in a Socialist Economy* (published in the UK by Cambridge University Press), was also translated and published in English in Nigeria. Again, I have made minor stylistic improvements. Throughout I have altered the symbols used in equations to make them consistent with those used in Kalecki's *Selected Essays on the Economic Growth of the Socialist and the Mixed Economy*.[29]

The numbered notes at the end are explanatory notes which I have added. The footnotes appearing at the bottom of the page in the text are Kalecki's own original notes. I have, however, added to the text a rather more extended explanatory note in the second half of the essay on the 'Problems in the Theory of Growth of a Socialist Economy'.

Finally, I must express my gratitude for the help and advice given to me by Dr Jerzy Osiatyński, the editor of Kalecki's Collected Works, who also made available to me the manuscript of his book *Michał Kalecki on a Socialist Economy* (Macmillan, forthcoming). In writing my own notes, I have made use of his excellent and extensive bibliographic notes in the third volume of the Colleted Works.

I would also like to thank Mrs Adela Kalecka for the kindness and encouragement with which she gave permission for this publication.

Thanks are also due to the British Academy for including me in their exchange scheme with the Polish Academy of Sciences in March 1985, thus enabling me to obtain valuable advice and information from Dr Osiatyński and Mrs Kalecka. Many others have contributed to my part in the publication of these essays when morale and patience were flagging. Needless to say, all errors of translation and interpretation and the views expressed in this introduction, where they are not expressly attributed to Kalecki, are mine.

2 The Essentials for Democratic Planning*

The idea of a planned economy finds favour today in many circles. Its sponsors include not only socialists, but also progressive Tories, neo-Liberals, and monopoly-capitalists. The middle, mainly intellectual groups, including some Labour intellectuals, tend to think of planning in the abstract – they generally fail to distinguish clearly between different kinds of planning, serving different objectives, and they regard it as essentially a technical operation, to be achieved by intellectual persuasion and some kind of simple basic control, such as State direction of credit-creation and investment. It is important to realise, however, that in the final outcome both the objectives and the methods of planning will be determined by the character of the political and social forces by which it will be directed, and that the real choice lies between socialist planning and monopoly-capitalist planning.

Two kinds of planning

It is therefore of primary importance for the Labour Party to make clear that it stands for *democratic* planning – and to draw all the necessary conclusions, in policy and action, from what is implied by the word 'democratic'. First, as to the objective, democratic planning implies planning for the maximum long-term satisfaction of the needs of the whole community, as against planning for a maximum long-term return to the owners of industry, which would be the aim of monopoly-capitalist planning. This means that while any form of planning for full

* First published in *Labour Discussion Notes*, no. 35 September 1942.

employment must ensure that at any given time there is a correct balance between the production of capital goods and consumption goods, socialist planning alone will have as its aim the full utilisation of all resources for the common good. Monopoly-capitalist planning, on the other hand, in the search for a stable return (profit and interest) over a long period, will often deliberately restrict both actual production and the application of new processes and techniques to industry. Secondly, as to method, democratic planning must satisfy the need of the producers (workers, technicians and managers) for some control over the activities in which they are engaged and some opportunity for creative initiative, i.e., for industrial democracy. Monopoly-capitalist planning, on the other hand, would inevitably be coloured by the owners' desire to retain their positions of command, and to increase their personal power, i.e., it would favour economic and social autocracy. It follows from the above that democratic planning must be directed by a state machine and a government which genuinely represents the interests of the main mass of working-consumers, whereas monopoly-capitalist planning would be controlled either directly by the leaders of big business and finance or by a state machine and a government which, however democratic in form, would in fact be subservient to their interests.

In drawing up Labour propaganda and, still more, a plan of action for a Labour government, it is therefore important to keep clearly in mind that democratic socialist planning will not merely be resisted by individualist capitalists seeking a return to a *laissez-faire*, competitive economy. It will be opposed still more by the powerful monopoly-capitalist groups, who will fight against it in two ways: positively, by working energetically to get their own kind of planning adopted, and negatively, by resisting encroachments on their economic and social power.

Labour must have no illusions about the great fight which will have to be waged against these groups. They will resist fiercely because what is at stake is not so much their profits as their personal and social power, which takes two forms: power in society as a whole, and power over workers in industry. As long as the first form of power remains, all the efforts of the workers in the factories and through the trade unions to diminish the second form of power can only have limited success. The fight for workers' rights in industry and for more effective workers' representation, through such things as works' councils and production committees, is, of course, of very great importance and, as we shall show later, it has a vital part to play in the *total* struggle against the capitalists. But it can never be a *substitute* for the necessary political fight to destroy the power wielded over society as a whole by the great capitalist interest-groups.

These great groups – the banks and insurance companies, the iron and steel trades, the big trusts and combines like Imperial Chemicals, Unilever, Courtaulds, General Electric, the oil and rubber companies, and so on – are today great independent societies which constitute a state (or a series of states) within the state, subject to their own internal laws and agreements and able, by their own decisions, to control the lives of millions of human beings. Their economic power is supported by the social and political power which they exercise through innumerable personal contacts in other branches of industry and commerce, in the Tory Party, in the Civil Service, in the higher ranks of the armed forces, the judiciary and the professions – in short, all that forms part of the complex which we call 'the ruling classes'. Their power is, in fact, a *class power* and, as long as this class power remains unbroken, the ability of the leading capitalist groups to run things in their way – and, at worst, to sabotage – is enormous. This power can be exercised in a variety of subtle ways which no formal laws – no mere legislative decisions of a Labour government, for example – can break. It can only be broken by destroying not merely their political influence, but what is its real basis, their economic power in the great productive forces over which they exercise practically unchallenged control.

First objectives of a socialist government

Here then must be Labour's first main objective after it has gained political power. Once the first elementary steps for the maintenance of the economic security of the workers have been taken, Labour will have to base its Plan of Action not on purely technical economic considerations, but on the aim of *changing the power relations in society*, by capturing the key centres of the economic, social and political power of the strongest capitalist groups. This means that the provisional order of priorities, as set out, for example, in such documents as 'Labour's Immediate Programme', may well have to be changed in favour of one conceived in terms of political and economic strategy.

Any national plan must inevitably provide for full central public control of banking and finance, investment and foreign trade, and possibly the allocation of basic raw materials and commodities. These measures, coupled with other measures of *indirect social control*, would provide a framework within which a good deal of scope could be left to private initiative, especially in the secondary and consumption industries and distribution. Yet, if our previous analysis is correct, these measures alone will not suffice to break the political and social power of the strongest capitalist groups. For them, nothing less than *direct social control* will be adequate. The form which this direct control takes must, of course, vary according to the type of industry or service, its present form of organisation, and so on. But the choice will generally lie between full nationalisation and some kind of public corporation. Wherever the latter form is chosen, however, the essential principle to be observed is that those who direct and manage the corporation shall have no financial interest in it other than their salaries and, conversely, that any private investors that there may be shall have no control over policy or management.

The policy of all the main groups in finance, industry and utilities must be coordinated and directed by some Central Economic Planning body which is responsible to Parliament.

Changing the power relationships in society

Yet, in the face of the powerful opposition which it will meet, no socialist government can hope to succeed unless its efforts are seconded by a feeling of a heightened tempo of development permeating the whole of society with, at its core, a mood of determination and, above all, of *self-confidence* amongst the workers and lower strata of society. Such a mood cannot be created artificially. It can be stimulated by propaganda, but only if a real basis for it exists.

Fortunately, such a basis *will* almost certainly exist. It will be created as a consequence of the success of those first elementary steps for the maintenance of full employment and economic security which, as we have said, must be taken by any socialist government. To put the matter in terms of a concrete situation, these steps will inevitably have to be taken by whatever government is in power during the immediate post-War period. For the creation of full employment and a sense of economic security will, once the inhibiting conditions of war are removed, fundamentally alter the internal power relationships within industry. With the sanction of the sack no longer operative, and with the workers freed from the more oppressive economic anxieties, the situation would become 'difficult' for the employers. There would be increasing interference by workers in management, and a new feeling of determination and self-confidence amongst the workers and the common people generally.

It is from this source that would arise the social pressure which would support and sustain a socialist government in its fight against the powerful capitalist groups and enable it to drive through its more radical planning measures. But these in their turn would react upon the situation within industry, giving still more power to the workers, encouraging them to make further demands and so further increasing the pressure from below.

The administrative measures from above and the pressure of the workers from below would thus interact with a cumulative effect, sustaining the impetus of the whole planning movement, and bringing about, in fact, a continuing social revolution. As the movement develops, new possibilities and new problems will arise, which will modify the course of the plan as it proceeds. It must therefore be sufficiently flexible to allow for variations as the situation demands. At the outset, we must have a clear idea of what we want to do and of what must be done, and there must be a rough scheme of priorities. But we must be ready to make changes as the changing social situation and the changing power relations within industry open up new possibilities and make new demands.

Once socialist planning is firmly established, the balance of power in industry will be much altered in favour of the workers that democratic forms are bound to develop in factories and society will lose its present rigid hierarchical structure. If this inevitable social content of our economic policy can be brought out and made clear to the masses in this country, then a great increase in faith and hope can be rallied behind a programme which, taken on its face value, might appear arid and academic. It would provide the moral element in Labour's appeal, as a complement to the material appeal of economic security.

The political task

The social pressure of the workers will itself, of course, create problems for a socialist government, especially in the industries which are not ripe for social control. The important thing, however, is that Labour should not be afraid of the consequences of the social revolution within industry, but should make itself master of the situation, not by trying to damp down the mood of the workers, as did the leaders of the Popular

Front in France, but by directing it against the opponents of democratic planning. The latter will of course be aware of the danger confronting them. The more far sighted among them may even seek to use their political and economic power to destroy the primary condition of the workers' self-confidence – full employment and economic security. The captains of industry may recall with regret the power which they possessed in the days of alternating slump and boom, with their unstable labour conditions. While not desiring the return of full crisis, they might seek either to sabotage the plans of a Labour government by financial or other means, or, if they had political power, to establish a condition of 'controlled under-employment'.

The political conclusion to which this points is one which offers a definite challenge to the Labour Movement. Whatever may happen *during* the war, it is clearly vital that well before the post-war relief and reconstruction boom is over there should come into full political power a Labour or Labour-dominated government composed of vigorous and determined men who are prepared without delay to fight a decisive battle against the forces of monopoly-capitalism, and to establish secure control, on behalf of the nation, over the key centres of economic and social power. This period, which may be short, will be the one of maximum opportunity for Labour, when full employment has generated a self-confident feeling amongst the workers. Then will be the time to use Labour's political power to the full; to strike boldly and to strike hard. This will be the moment to lay the basis for that continuing social revolution without which democratic socialist planning will remain a sterile dream.

3 Workers' Councils and Central Planning*

I

During the final months of 1956, profound changes occurred in the manner in which the Polish economy is managed. These changes found their expression in three legislative documents: The Resolution of the Council of Ministers, extending the rights of state enterprises in industry, and the Laws on Workers' Councils and Factory Funds.[1] I shall not discuss these documents here in detail, since they are already well known. Instead I shall limit myself to setting out their essential contents.

The resolution extending the rights of industrial state enterprises radically reduces the number of compulsory targets that the enterprise will have in its annual plan. In addition, it leaves enterprises with much greater freedom in their other activities than they have had in the past.

The Workers' Councils Law entrusts these councils with the policy-making function in enterprises. The workers' council, chosen by the workforce, decides about the general lines of development for the enterprise. The director of the enterprise is bound by the decisions of the council, but retains managerial discretion in carrying them out. The director himself is nominated by the relevant state authority, but must be approved by the workers' council. The council can also propose his dismissal.

Finally, the Factory Funds Law creates the basis for giving the workforce a material interest in the rational conduct of the enterprise. For the time being this is only outline legislation. The individual

* First published in *Nowe Drogi*, 1956.

ministries are to devise in the near future the actual system of financing the factory fund, which may be different in the various sectors of production. In each case a different method of financing may need to be considered in order to ensure that the supply of consumer goods is automatically increased to balance the benefits paid out to the workforce.[2]

It is clear that this legislation constitutes an organic whole. The extension of enterprise autonomy gives workers' councils the possibility of displaying initiative in the organisation of production, and the enterprise fund law creates the material incentives to encourage such initiatives. It should also be mentioned that, despite the important simplification of central planning, as in the past it still sends instructions to the enterprise regarding the most important features of its activity. In particular, the central planners still set down for the enterprise its targeted value of production, the total amount of the latter and its most important commodity groups, and the wage fund. Furthermore, despite the considerable decentralisation of renovation and similar investment decisions, the central authorities continue to decide on the construction of the larger investment projects. Finally, prices continue to be centrally determined, and basic materials are allocated on the basis of centrally defined criteria through the appropriate administrative hierarchy at each level in the economy.

Thus the essential structure of economic organisation that is emerging after the most recent reforms consists of enterprises directed by workers' councils which operate within the framework of central planning in the strict sense of the term. In its present form, this system is undoubtedly incomplete. On the one hand, even if we leave aside the question of further loosening the constraints of central planning, there can be no doubt that certain plan targets should be improved. For instance, the general drawbacks of using gross output as a plan target are widely known.[3] A better indicator would undoubtedly be the value of net marketed output at factory prices, i.e., the value of sales at factory-gate prices, after deducting the value of bought-in materials and components.[4] On the other hand, where the limits of planning are concerned, there is little doubt that co-operatives and industrial enterprises of purely local importance should be excluded to a great extent from the scope of the central plan and administered in a manner more similar to the Jugoslav model.

However, in spite of the fact that the present system is still incomplete, and in spite of uncertainty about its final form, it is worth asking now whether a structure of economic organisation which relies on a synthesis of workers' councils and central planning, and which has emerged rather spontaneously, is desirable, from the economic and social point of view, and whether it is viable. Furthermore, what are the benefits of replacing the old system of management with this new structure?

II

In my opinion, the structure under discussion is economically and socially desirable because both of its constituent elements, i.e., central planning and workers' councils, appear to be indispensable for rapid economic development which would nevertheless be free from the distortions that characterised recent economic management. The existence of workers' councils would guarantee the elimination of such aberrations. The councils would perform the following three functions:

1. As an authority directly responsible to the workforce, they would prevent abuses of conditions of work and overtime payments, and similar impositions of past years.
2. They would counteract the tendency towards excessive bureaucratisation and centralisation of the economy, since their resistance to this would be far more effective than that of enterprise directors who owe their appointment to the central authorities.
3. Finally, given the appropriate material incentives, their close contact with the workforce would release initiative which it is impossible to inspire by central planning.

The need for central planning is now questioned perhaps more than the importance of workers' councils. No one surely would dispense with the central planning altogether. However, essentially this is not a very meaningful statement, since the notion of planning can be so diluted as to embrace even counter-cyclical intervention in the capitalist countries. What we have in mind here is central planning in the sense that we gave it above, i.e., planning that embraces the volume of production, the wage fund, larger investment projects, as well as control over prices and the distribution of basic materials. More than one person will certainly disagree with such a notion of planning, believing that it would shackle enterprise and paralyse the activity of workers' councils.

For instance, it is often argued that central planning of the volume of production is futile: it ought to be replaced by such incentives as would induce enterprises to make the fullest possible use of their productive potential. A quite common opinion has it that this incentive function could be performed by a system in which the workforce would have a share in the profits of the enterprise. But it is easy to show that in a socialist economy the implementation of this principle would come up against a number of serious complications and difficulties.

In the first place, since the ratio of profits to the wage fund will vary between enterprises, it will be necessary to establish the percentage share of profits that will be distributed to the workforce on a differentiated basis. This will be necessary to avoid serious anomalies in workers' earnings arising in different industries, or even in different factories in the same industry. But even this would meet with problems. If a factory is mis-managed, as a result of which its profits are small, then clearly it would not be justifiable to secure for the workers a higher share of the profits, in order to equalise their earnings with those of other workers. If, however, the low profits are the result of the factory's technological backwardness, then there is no reason why its workforce should therefore be penalised. Of course this situation will be constantly changing. Thus the process of fixing the workforces' share of profits in such a way as to maintain some social justice will be a very complicated undertaking.

Secondly, the significance of the workers' share in profits as a material incentive is limited because incomes from this source cannot be established at a level that is too high in relation to basic wages. If this were to happen, workers' incomes would fluctuate considerably, which would be very undesirable. But if their share in profits does not constitute quite a substantial part of the income of the workforce, then it is difficult to see how this incentive can become the panacea ensuring the efficient functioning of the enterprise.

Thirdly, profits depend not only on the volume of output, but also, and often to a greater degree, on costs. The possibility cannot be excluded that the efforts of the enterprise may be directed not so much towards increasing production as towards reducing costs. In some cases this may be desirable. But in others the result may be wholly undesirable from the point of view of the economy as a whole. If, for instance, the enterprise has an excessively large labour force in relation to raw material supplies or its productive capacity, then the main emphasis will be on reducing labour costs. This will bring about a rise in unemployment, rather than an increase in per capita national income. Profits are a synthetic indicator[5] of enterprise performance. Therein lies their strength, but also their weakness, as an indicator.

It is worth noting that all these difficulties in applying the concept of profit-sharing arise out of the very nature of a socialist society. In a capitalist society, no one is bothered if capitalists in different industries or in different enterprises in the same industry are 'unjustly' rewarded. Furthermore, fluctuations in the income of capitalists do not in any way have the same kind of severe adverse effects as would fluctuations in workers' incomes, were these to depend on profit-sharing. This is for the simple reason that capitalists invest a large part of their profits. Hence, even significant changes in profits may not affect the consumption of capitalists. Finally, in a capitalist society, profits are not some synthetic indicator, but the very purpose of enterprise activity.

It should be stated that the above argument is of a rather fundamental character. In the conditions obtaining at present in Poland, profits can be raised without an increase in production and without reducing costs, by changing the composition of output in favour of goods whose profit margin is greater because of a distorted system of prices. But even if these distortions were removed, the reliance of the economy solely on enterprise profit-sharing would not necessarily guarantee rapid economic progress.

III

Let us now consider other elements of central planning, in particular the control of prices and the allocation of basic materials. It is often thought that the fixing of prices by the central authorities is merely unnecessary bureaucratic interference, and that the best regulator of prices is the process of 'free competition'. However, as in the present-day capitalist system, prices would then be fixed by overt or tacit agreements between enterprises. This would indeed be the easiest way to achieve high profits. At the same time, it would create a tendency to restrict rather than expand the volume of production.

In fact the idea of letting enterprises fix prices freely does not have too many supporters. However, far more widespread is the opposition to the 'administrative' allocation of materials. Instead it is argued that materials should be distributed by means of a flexible pricing policy pursued by the central authorities. Thus, an inadequate supply of some materials should be balanced with demand by an appropriate increase in prices. Accordingly, in this way bureaucratic allocation at all levels of the economy ought to be replaced by 'economic' instruments.

Like many such theories, this one also sounds much better when formulated in general terms than when it is applied to actual situations. For example, let us suppose that as a result of an underfulfilment of the plan targets for rolled steel production, an acute shortage of these products has appeared. What effect will an increase in the price of rolled steel then have? As a consequence of raising the price of this basic material, it will be necessary to raise correspondingly the prices of investment goods which use rolled steel in their manufacture, e.g., machines, boilers and freight wagons, as well as such consumer durables as passenger cars. Unless the funds assigned for investment are increased, an increase in the price of investment goods will reduce investment in individual sectors of the economy. However, it will be difficult to anticipate to what degree these reductions in investment will induce a fall in the demand for steel.

A similar situation will arise with consumer durables. An increase in their prices will induce a reduction in the demand for them. But it will be difficult to foresee its extent of the reduction in demand, or how soon it will occur. To make demand equal to the reduced supply, it will be necessary to raise prices by as much as will induce a sufficient reduction in demand for investment goods and consumer durables. This may only be achieved by successive approximations. At the same time, if there is no significant reduction in some highly steel-intensive sectors of industry, such as those producing railway carriages or motor cars, then the general reduction in investment and consumption may have to be quite substantial. Reaching such an equilibrium may also take a long time, during which demand will exceed supply, and therefore stocks will be run down.

A much simpler and effective procedure would be to restrict investment, taking into account general economic priorities as well as the steel-intensity of particular investment goods. The consumption of consumer durables would be reduced similarly. In the latter case, their prices are raised by increasing turnover tax to the level at which demand will approximately balance with the reduced supply. Obviously production plans in particular industries will be modified as will also be their supply of steel.

If this shortage is of a permanent character, then even while using the method outlined above, an increase in the price of rolled steel is advisable in any case. We presume that there will be some kind of incentive system to encourage savings in the material costs of current production as well as in investment. In such circumstances, an increase in the price of steel would induce the substitution of other materials, where this is possible.

There is the question of how this equilibrating mechanism proceeds in capitalist countries. In general, in developed capitalist countries there exist unused productive reserves. Therefore, increases in production play the decisive part there in balancing supply with demand. However, when this mechanism fails, as it did during the last War, or even during the period of rapid rearmament between 1950 and 1953, contemporary capitalism also resorts to administrative distribution according to priorities decided by the government.

In concluding our discussion on the effectiveness of central planning, it should be borne in mind that the demands made upon it will be the greater the faster the rate of economic growth and the increase in consumption. This is because, in such circumstances, contradictions arise between the standard of living in the longer term, and the share of consumption in national income in the short term. The desire to moderate these contradictions leads to the mobilisation of all resources, with the result that the economy becomes strained. In any case, with rapid economic development, it is generally more likely that there will be inadequate coordination of the activity in different sectors of the economy, leading to bottlenecks. In particular, an imbalance between import requirements and achievable export performance may easily appear. It is clear that an economy facing these problems requires stricter central planning than a stagnant or slowly developing economy. Thus, the rejection of central planning in the sense defined above implies either abandoning rapid economic development, or dependence on permanent foreign assistance.

IV

We concluded above that a synthesis of central planning and workers' councils is desirable. This of course does not mean that such a system is necessarily viable, but in any case, it does create the basis for efforts to secure its viability.

One should not be deluded into thinking that such arrangements are free from inconsistencies and easy to operate. Undoubtedly there will always be a tendency in them to reduce the prerogatives of the workers' councils in favour of greater centralisation, as well as a tendency for workers' councils to weaken the central plan. On the one hand, there will exist the danger of weakening the position of the workers' councils and bureaucratising the whole system of management. On the other hand, pressure from the workers' councils may lead to a situation in which it will be necessary to slow the pace of economic development or become dependent on foreign aid. Alternatively, after a period of chaos, 'order' will be restored with a return to a system of bureaucratic centralism.

Here I would like to point out that already after these few months, a weakening of central planning, to the benefit of the workers' councils, has occurred that contains a serious danger for the economy. I have in mind specifically the renunciation of all controls over employment. In accordance with the resolution extending their rights, enterprises' compulsory plan targets include their total annual wage bill, but exclude their average wage and the numbers employed. In many factories in manufacturing industries, the supply of raw materials is the factor limiting production and constraining the growth of labour productivity. In practice, therefore, cost-cutting may lead to substantial reductions in employment. For, with a given supply of raw materials, those workers remaining in employment will be able to obtain higher earnings, especially if they are on piece-work. At the same time, the enterprise profit-sharing fund, which increases with cost-savings and/or profit increases, will grow.

However, no matter how much labour productivity may thereby rise in an enterprise, the incomes of the population as a whole will not increase. This is because the growth in labour productivity at the plant level will be counterbalanced by increased unemployment outside it. Indeed, because of the above-mentioned difficulties with raw material supplies, it will not be possible to re-employ workers made redundant by some manufacturing enterprises in other plants. Moreover, it is doubtful whether the unemployed will direct themselves precisely to those areas where there are labour shortages, i.e., to coal-mining and state farms.[6] It should also be noted that their eventual re-employment in schemes of public works could not be financed wholly by taxing the more productive enterprises. This is because a significant proportion of the wage costs saved at the plant level by reducing employment would be swallowed up by the increased earnings of those who remained at work.

In these circumstances, it is absolutely necessary, in my view, for the central authorities to resist excessive reductions in employment. At the same time, they should encourage workers, rather than taking the line of least resistance, to direct their ingenuity towards saving raw materials, reducing faulty production, designing products that use more labour and relatively abundant raw materials, and finally undertaking for export, production from which the proceeds would pay for the materials used. All these measures will enable the enterprise to increase useful production with a given supply of deficit raw materials and without reducing employment. In this case, an increase in labour productivity at the factory level will be equivalent to an increase in per capita national income.

In order to avoid misunderstandings, it is worth mentioning that the unemployment discussed here is something completely different to the unemployment that is found in capitalist countries. The former is caused by a surplus of labour, relative to the attainable supply of raw materials, rather than insufficient demand.[7]

V

We may now consider the question of whether the extension of enterprise autonomy and the creation of workers' councils will contribute to increasing living standards in the next few years. In considering this question, it is necessary to distinguish between mining and extractive industries on the one hand, and manufacturing industries on the other. In the former, an appropriate system of incentives would undoubtedly contribute to increased production. This in turn would help to solve many economic difficulties and thereby increase living standards. For instance, an increase in the rate of extraction of coal would allow more of it to be exported. The additional foreign exchange could be used to purchase raw materials for those industries producing consumer goods, or even foodstuffs. Similarly, an increase in the production of building materials would allow their sales in rural areas to be increased. This would directly stimulate the expansion of agricultural production.[8] Moreover, by improving the condition of agricultural buildings, a greater supply of building materials in rural areas helps to create the basis for increased agricultural production in the future.

However, as a result of the system of incentives that is used at present in these industries, productivity within them is fairly high. Further substantial increases in their output would require both considerable investment, and the recruitment of additional labour. The latter would, in the case of coal-mining for instance, encounter serious difficulties.[9]

In the manufacturing industries, production depends to a large degree on raw material supplies. These in turn are limited by the constraints on the amounts that may be imported, and on the possible expansion of agriculture. As we have already mentioned, in these industries, it is often relatively easy to increase labour productivity. However, this tends to lead to reductions in employment rather than increases in output. By using the appropriate incentives, it is nevertheless possible to induce the workforce to concentrate their efforts on economizing on raw materials, eliminating waste, and expanding export production. But however significant may be the increases in output that can be obtained by these efforts, one should not expect miracles here, with given supplies of raw materials, especially in the short term. In the near future the new system of management will only gradually become effective. Only after some time will its advantages become apparent.

Undoubtedly, in the longer term, workers' councils which counteract the bureaucratisation of the central planning system, but do not undermine it, can bring about significant benefits through releasing the creative initiatives that are shackled in a totally centralised system. However, in the short term, the key factors on which living standards depend are the priorities for economic development that are laid down in the central plans. Especially crucial among them are the provisions in respect of the structure of investment, foreign trade and agricultural development. One should not therefore expect better results from reforms in economic management than they can give even under the most favourable circumstances.

Nevertheless, irrespective of its economic benefits, the establishment of workers' councils should be considered an essential part of creating a system of democratic socialism.

Appendix[10]

The Workers' Council Law sets as its guiding principle 'the realisation of working-class initiative to participate in enterprise management'. To this end, workers' councils are established in those state enterprises in which a majority of workers so decides.

The functions and powers of Workers' Councils

'The Workers' Council acts on behalf of the workforce of an enterprise that is national property.' Within the framework of the legal statutes in force and the enterprise's obligations under the national economic plan, the Council's activities are as follows:

(a) The appraisal and acceptance of the enterprise's annual production plans.

(b) Setting targets for improvements in the efficiency of production (increases in labour productivity, improvements in the quality of production, economies in the use of raw materials, fuel and equipment, etc.).

(c) The determination, within the limits of the enterprise's legal powers and national collective agreements, of conditions of employment (health and safety at work, production quotas, rates of pay and the bonuses related to them, internal enterprise regulations).

(d) Approval of the enterprise's annual report and accounts.

(e) The distribution among the workforce of their share of enterprise profits (i.e., the so-called Enterprise Fund. A separate law stipulates that its total value may not exceed 8½% of the enterprise's wage fund. The Enterprise Fund may be distributed among the workforce in the form of bonuses, or assigned to housing construction.[11] A general meeting of the whole workforce is supposed to decide on this distribution of the Fund).

(f) In some cases consulting the whole workforce by means of a ballot.

The Workers' Council

The Workers' Council shall be set up according to the following general guidelines:

(a) The Council shall be elected by means of a secret ballot of the operatives, engineers, technicians, professional staff and other workers of the enterprise.

(b) Where possible, at least two-thirds of the Council should be shop-floor workers.

(c) The Council is responsible for its actions to the enterprise's workforce, to which it is obliged to report, and by which it may be recalled. Every worker of the enterprise has the right to participate in meetings of the Council.

(d) The members of the Council have the right to be reimbursed for earnings lost in the course of carrying out their responsibilities.

Relations with the Trades Union Committee

Decisions of the Workers' Council which affect conditions of employment may be accepted only in agreement with the Trades Union Committee.[12] In the event of disagreement between the two, the matter shall be decided by the whole workforce.

Relations with the Enterprise Director

1. The Enterprise Director is a member of the Workers' Council, but may not be its Chairman or Vice-Chairman. The Director has a duty to prepare and submit to the Council all the information that may be necessary for its work.
2. The Director is appointed and recalled by the relevant state authorities, after approval of the decision by the Workers' Council. The Council has the right to propose the appointment or dismissal of the Director.
3. The Director directs the enterprise's operations and is legally responsible for them. In relation to the workforce, he is in charge of every employee of the enterprise. Outside meetings of the Council, its members have no authority beyond that which may arise from the job that they hold in the enterprise.
4. The Director is responsible for his work both to the Workers' Council and to the relevant state authorities. He may not issue instructions or give orders that do not conform with the plan, the decisions of the Workers' Council, or instructions from the state authorities.
5. The Director has a duty to prevent the carrying out of a decision of the Workers' Council if it is incompatible with the law or the economic plan. In cases of emergency, the Director has the right to take decisions which fall within the area of competence of the Workers' Council, if this is necessary for the normal functioning of the enterprise. In both of these cases he should inform the Council of his action.

6. In the event of an intractable disagreement arising between the Director and the Workers' Council both parties should appeal to the state authority which is in charge of the enterprise. If this appeal does not resolve the issue, then they have the right of appeal to the relevant Minister.

4 The Vertically Integrated Firm as an Element in the New Economic Model*

The discussion around the new economic model has demonstrated the fundamental role that is played in it by the relationship between the newly autonomous enterprises and their superior authority, which is to take the place of the existing central boards.[1] It is easy to see the implications of this issue are much broader. Up to now, the discussion about 'directives' and 'incentives' as instruments of central planning has been to a large degree abstracted from the character of the agency directly superior to the enterprise. Nevertheless, these two matters are closely related. The way in which instructions and incentives are arranged, and especially the ease with which they can be differentiated between particular branches of industry, depends to a large degree on the character of the intermediate agencies between the central planning authorities and the individual enterprises. Closely linked to this is another problem, namely that of technical co-operation, and specifically the distribution of industrial supplies.

It is frequently argued that the present central boards should be replaced by associations of their subsidiary enterprises. It needs to be stated that this solution does not introduce anything new other than transferring enterprise autonomy onto the next level above. At the same time, certain undesirable features may emerge. The association of enterprises would, by its nature, have a character similar to that of a cartel. Obviously, if the central authorities in the reformed economy keep their function of setting prices, then the monopolistic tendencies of these associations will not be able to emerge in this domain. However, it is not possible altogether to exclude attempts at joint reductions in

* First published in *Polityka*, no. 8 April 1957, 17–23.

planned production, coordinated demands for higher material supplies per unit of output, and similar pressures.

It seems to me that a much more positive approach would be to set up vertically integrated firms. By this I mean large economic units that would be, where possible, self-sufficient in materials. They may therefore include, for instance, steel foundries and machine tools manufacturers. Clearly, such firms would hardly ever be wholly self-sufficient, and they would normally buy and sell some semi-fabricates. Nevertheless, the ingenious structuring of such firms may substantially simplify the business of technical co-operation and industrial supply.

Regarding horizontal integration, the firm ought not necessarily to include all the enterprises producing a particular type of final output. On the contrary, the existence of a number of such firms would counteract tendencies towards monopoly.

The individual enterprises within the firm would retain a high degree of monopoly. The central authorities would not interfere at all in the internal affairs of the firm, dealing exclusively with its external supplies and the results of its operations as a whole. The firm therefore would influence the enterprises within it by means of the instructions and incentives which it is empowered to enact, and which could be adapted to the specific operating conditions of its enterprises.

At the same time, all the directives and incentives applied to the firm by its superior authority would be based on indicators relating to its 'external' activities, such as total sales, or the profits from all of its operations. The sums that the firm would receive in the form of premia,[2] its share of overall profits or above-plan profits, etc., would serve to finance material incentives for the constituent enterprises as well as for the firm's management.

Thus there would be strong financial links between the firm as a whole and the individual enterprises that make it up. The better the firm organises coordinates between its constituent enterprises, the better overall results it will achieve, and the greater the funds that it will have at its disposal to distribute to its enterprises in the form of bonuses, shares in profits, etc. But the firm's overal results would obviously depend on the achievements of the individual enterprises.

Regarding the manner in which the firms are managed, it seems to me that this should be analogous to the present method of enterprise management, albeit with certain modifications. Just as in the enterprise, there should be a firm council, whose members would include representatives of the workers' councils of the individual enterprises.

This council would decide on the overall policy of the firm. However, the day to day running of the firm would be the responsibility of the firm's managers, who would be equivalent to the director of an enterprise. At the same time, because the firm would be more directly associated with the central planning authorities, it would be desirable to have representatives of the firm's central board on the firm's council, and perhaps even a representative of the authority that is directly responsible for the firm.

The above analysis shows that vertically integrated firms would have the following advantages:

(1) There would exist a community of interests between the management of the firm and the individual enterprises. This would facilitate the efficient management of the firm by its council and directors.

(2) Within each firm, it would be possible to apply those instructions and incentives that are best suited to the specific operating conditions of its subsidiary enterprises. The character of these directives and incentives would be decided solely by the firm, and could be changed from year to year without reducing their effectiveness.

(3) In their management of the economy, the central authorities would have to deal with only a relatively small number of firms. They would also be able to apply to those firms differentiated directives and incentives. This would greatly simplify and extend the flexibility of economic administration.

(4) However, the greatest advantage would be obtained in simplifying technical co-operation and materials' supplies.

5 Outline of a New System of Incentives and Directives*

The purpose of this essay is to sketch out a system according to which an enterprise would function in a reformed scheme of economic management. In my view, the essential elements of this system would be:

(a) Net output. This would be the basic plan indicator of enterprise activity.

(b) The wage fund limit. Net output would be the decisive factor in setting this.

(c) Variations in profits, i.e., the increase in profit relative to its level in the preceding period. On this basis, 'supplementary payments' would be made to the enterprise.

(d) Factory prices and the principles determining them.[1] These would ensure that incentives in the wages fund and the 'supplementary payments' operated properly.

(e) Interest-bearing, non-repayable, investment credits.

Net output

By net output we mean the difference between the value of total output at factory prices, and the cost at purchase price of those materials, fuel and externally sourced components used in production. We assume that each enterprise will receive from its superior authorities a plan of net output which it is supposed to carry out. This plan will be calculated according to the previous year's output and materials' prices.

Two methods may be used in calculating net output. One consists of

* First published in *Życie Gospodarcze*, no. 29 21 July 1959.

comparing the value of net output according to the prices prevailing in the base, and deducting from that the value of materials, etc., in that same period's prices. The second method consists of counting up the value of production measured in 'net prices' of that base period, that is, according to the difference between the prices and the unit costs of materials etc., in that period. The first method allows for increases in net output and the saving of materials, whether planned or actual in the final outcome. These factors cannot be taken into account in using the second method.

We shall assume that the first method is used, since it is simpler to operate. Moreover, allowing for materials' saving gives the net output indicator more of an overall, synthetic character. With this assumption the enterprise may achieve increases in net output not only by increasing production, but also by economising on materials used.

Although we are presuming that the net output indicator will be relayed to the enterprise by the agency in charge of it as a plan directive, in contrast to the present arrangements no material benefit for the enterprise will be attached to the fulfilment or overfulfilment of the plan in our proposed system. The only guarantee that the production plan will be carried out will be the formal responsibility of the management, which will have the right to demand that the workers' council co-operates in carrying out this plan. In any case, as we shall see, the incentives that we propose will have the effect of increasing net output, and therefore encouraging the fulfilment and even the overfulfilment of the plan.

The wage fund limit

We propose that the limit on the wages fund of the enterprise for a given year should be calculated as follows:

First of all, the auditors would compute the size of the enterprise's wage fund for the past year, on the basis of the wage rates in force at the start of that year under collective agreements. The proposed wage fund limit would be the previous year's wage fund so calculated, raised in proportion to the actual increase in net output, relative to the previous year's net output. This wage fund will as a rule be greater than would be warranted by the increase in employment and piece-work earnings. However, the surplus will not be deducted, but will be used to finance the payment of various kinds of bonuses to be established within the enterprise, for instance, bonuses for the technical and administrative staff, bonuses for material savings, etc.

In this way, the very method of determining the limit on the wage fund will act as an incentive to increase net output with a given labour force. However, there is lacking here any incentive to secure increases in net output by increasing employment, since in general the size of the wages fund per employee would not be enlarged by this. Therefore this incentive needs to be supplemented by another one which would provide significant benefits for the existing labour force against increases in employment as well. As we shall see, such an incentive is provided by the workers' share in increases in profits.

Labour's share in profit increase

This part of the scheme depends in principle on comparing profits in a given year, also calculated using the value of production at factory prices, with the total profits achieved in the previous year. The difference between the two would form the basis of 'supplementary payments', i.e., payments in addition to earnings in the form of bonuses for the technical and administrative staff, or from the factory fund.[2] Supplementary payments would therefore constitute a particular proportion of that increase in profits. It is easy to show that this incentive will produce a strong tendency to increase total net output, and not just average net output per worker. Essentially, it will be possible to achieve an increase in profits, by enlarging employment relative to the previous year, and this profit increase would be the source of the supplementary payments. Every member of the workforce will therefore benefit from increasing employment. If the number employed in the previous year amounted to n persons, the rise in employment is Δn, and the resulting increment in profits totalled Δp, then the basis for the supplementary payments made under this title per employee would be:

$$\frac{\Delta p}{n+\Delta n}$$

However, our discussion of this issue does not finish here. In order that the rise in profits should be matched by increases in net output and generally measure the improved performance of the enterprise, it is necessary to correct it for factors that are independent of the effort put in by the workforce, such as, primarily, changes in the prices of finished products, prices of materials and wage rates. Obviously, when the price of final output is increased to compensate for these changes, then the problem does not arise.

One other difficulty needs to be allowed for. The scheme put forward here would have the effect of making the additional earnings of the workforce dependent on a factor that is rather unstable. The change in profits will be extremely sensitive to all kinds of fortuitous occurrences, such as irregular deliveries of raw materials. In view of this, it would be desirable to have as the basis of the supplementary payments not the adjusted rise in profits relative to the previous year, but rather the arithmetic mean of adjusted profit increase over, say, the last three years.

We can illustrate this as follows. Let us suppose that profits in year zero amounted to 100 million złoty, in the first year they reached zł.120 millions, in the second year they were zł.130 millions, and in the third year zł.120 millions. In this case, the change in profits in the first, second and third years amounted to zł.20, 10 and 15 millions respectively. In each year we would correct the increase in profits relative to the previous year for those changes in prices and wages that are independent of the enterprise's operations. Let us assume that the increase in profits thus adjusted equals zł.18, 8 and 16 millions in each of these years respectively. The average adjusted profits increase comes to zł.14 millions. If supplementary payments to the workforce are set at 50% of the increase in profits in each year, then they will receive in the third year zł.7 millions. It is clear that by calculating supplementary payments in this way, the effect of the greater profits achieved in a given year is more lasting, since it influences payments for the subsequent two years.

In principle, this profit is equal to net output minus the wage costs, depreciation and the interest actually paid on credits. But again, in practice this is not strictly correct. Net output also includes the increase in stocks held over the period under review. However, profit should only be reckoned on output sold. In this way an incentive for marketing production is created. Basing the wage fund total on net output does not provide such an incentive.

It should also be noted that the proportion of the increase in profits that is paid out to the workforce may, and in some cases must be, varied. For example, after a period during which existing productive reserves are brought into use, further increases in profits may only be attained at a slower pace. In these circumstances it would be desirable to increase the share of supplementary payments in the profits increase.

The principles for setting factory prices

The way in which factory prices are determined influences fundamentally the operation of the incentives embodied in the limit placed on the wage bill, and in the supplementary payments. This influence works in various ways.

First of all, differences in percentage profit margins between various commodities produced by a given enterprise can lead to undesirable shifts in the commodity mix of its output.

Secondly, the size of that margin determines the relationship between cost reductions or production increases and changes in profits. Thus it influences the relative effectiveness of incentives towards reducing cost and towards expanding output. Essentially, with constant unit costs, the rise in profits is in proportion to the percentage increase in production and the size of that margin. With a constant level of production, the increase in profits is in proportion to percentage reductions in costs and does not depend on the magnitude of that margin. Therefore, the greater is that margin, the more effective is the incentive to increase production, relative to the incentive to reduce costs.[3]

These considerations lead to the following rules for determining factory prices.

First, care should be taken where possible to keep the profit margin on costs at the same level for all the products of a given industry, in order to avoid a running down of production of less profitable items. This principle should be strictly adhered to, especially in the initial period of realising longer term plans. In this period, factory prices should be allowed to vary at least to allow for changes in material costs and official wage rates which can seriously disturb the uniformity of profit margins. Disparities of this kind, which arise from unequal growth in productivity, are usually less serious because of the slow pace at which productivity rises and its tendency to affect equally the whole range of a firm's output. Obviously in cases where there is a need to accelerate the production of a particular commodity, its profit margin can be set on purpose at a level that is higher than that for other products.

At the same time, profit margins should be differentiated in different industries. They should be set higher for those industries where, relative to other industries, increases in production are more important than reductions in costs.

Investment and interest-bearing credits

The interest of the workforce in increasing its enterprise's profits will obviously act as an incentive to investment. However, from the point of view of the economy as a whole, increasing output or reducing costs where possible by means of small investment outlays, is more advantageous.

In view of this, the investment grants hitherto made should be treated as non-repayable credits on which interest should be paid. Some part of the depreciation fund would remain at the disposal of the enterprise and another portion of it would be paid in to central funds. This reduction in the retained depreciation fund would allow for the fact that, in practice, the whole of fixed capital is not generally reconstructed in its original form. Only that part of the depreciation fund which is kept by the enterprise should therefore be used for renovation and modernisation. But the enterprise would receive from the government interest on that part of the depreciation fund that is paid to the state. This would enable the enterprise to reduce its interest payments to the state for investment credits. Similarly, the enterprise would get interest at the same rate on that part of its depreciation funds which it does not use up. The same would apply to the sums realised by the enterprise through the sale of plant and equipment that is surplus to its requirements.

The above remarks apply to investments planned and controlled by the central authorities. Apart from this there would be a decentralised investment fund from which investment credits would be advanced to enterprises according to banking criteria. The rate of interest in this case would be the equilibrium rate that equalises the sums ear-marked for decentralised investments and the demand for such credits. The rate would therefore always be subject to change. The principles governing depreciation would remain the same as those for centralised investments. (Non-repayment of credits seems to me to be a considerably simpler arrangement than one in which the enterprise simultaneously repays credits, pays interest and defrays the costs of amortisation.)

It remains for us to consider how the process of investment would be incorporated into the system of enterprise functioning outlined above.

If an enterprise invests, then it will only gain the benefit of this as long as the new capacity provides an increase in profits. After profits stabilise at the new level, this benefit will cease. Allowing for the use of the *average* increase in profits over a few years as the basis for supplementary payments, then, strictly speaking, the benefit will cease only a few years after profits have stabilized. However, by the same process, the burden of interest payments will cease to have an effect on supplementary payments when capacity ceases to expand as a result of investment. This is because from this time the amount of interest paid remains at the same level, and therefore does not influence the increase in profits.

Concluding remarks

Our considerations have dealt with incentives and the instructions transmitted to the individual enterprise by the agency in charge of it. However, the situation would be substantially altered if enterprises were grouped into firms operating on the principles of economic accounting. Then the immediately superior authority for an enterprise would become an enormous enterprise. Incentives and instructions coming from the central authorities would be concerned with the operations of the integrated firm as a whole, its net output, its total wages costs and supplementary payments to all of its employees based on the increase in the total profits of its enterprises. At the same time, the instructions and incentives directed by the management of the firm to its constituent enterprises could, but need not necessarily, be of the same kind. It would be quite possible for individual firms to work out and apply 'for internal use' other systems which may be more appropriate to the peculiar circumstances of a given industry.

6 Central Price Determination as an Essential Feature of a Socialist Economy*

The following remarks, although purely theoretical, can be seen as a contribution to the discussion on the practical problems of operating market mechanisms in a socialist economy. We shall examine only three cases: the determination of prices in a contemporary capitalist economy; price formation in a socialist economy by the central authorities; and, finally, price-fixing in the latter type of economy, but by means of enterprise decision, in other words, in a decentralised way.

1. In the contemporary capitalist economy, the costs of production, to a greater degree than demand, determine prices. At the same time, the costs of production themselves are decided by monopolies and semi-monopolies. This kind of price determination influences the functioning of the capitalist system in such a way as to intensify depressions and business crises.

We may ask ourselves what kind of relations prevail in this system of monopolistic and semi-monopolistic price formation. In examining this question, the following assumptions are usually made:

(a) The economy is a closed one.

(b) The government has no economic functions and there are no taxes or government expenditure.

(c) The whole of national income is divided up into two components, Investment, I, and Consumption, C.

All economic activity can now be represented using a simple two-sector economic model. Sector I produces final investment goods, as

* First published as 'Centralistićko odredivanje cena kao bitni elemenat socijalistićke ekonomike: Drugo predavanje prof. dr. Mihaila Kaleckog, oderžano u Institutu za medunarodnu politiku i privredu,' in *Medžunarodni Problemi*, Belgrade, no. 3 1958 pp. 137–140, from a lecture taken down in shorthand by V. Trićkovicia.

well as the raw materials and semi-fabricates necessary for their manufacture. Sector II produces consumer goods. This formulation corresponds to Marx's scheme of reproduction, with one proviso. This is that sector I includes not only the production of means of production, but also preceding phases of production, up to the stage of raw materials extraction.

For the sake of simplicity, it is also assumed that:

(a) There are no savings.
(b) Consumption by capitalists remains constant.
(c) All daily periods of work change in the same proportion.
(d) Labour costs are constant, and prices are stable.

The assumption limiting capitalists' consumption may be removed without affecting our basic conclusions.

The following variables appear in the model:

I	Gross investment, or the value of sector I's output.
C	The value of consumer production, or the value of sector II's output.
ΔI	The increase in the value of investment goods, or the increase in the gross output of sector I.
ΔC	The increase in the value of consumer production, i.e., the increase in sector II's production.
$m_1 \Delta I$	That part of the increase in sector I's production that is equal to the increase in profits in sector I; in other words, the accumulated part of the increase in production.
$(1-m_1)\Delta I$	The increase in personal income (wages) of workers in sector I.
$m_2 \Delta C$	The accumulated part of the increase in the production of consumer goods (the increase in profits in sector II).
$(1-m_2)\Delta C$	The increase in the personal income (wages) of workers in sector II, equivalent to the rise in their consumption.

Coefficients m_1 and m_2 express the degree of monopolisation in each of the sectors. The question arises: what is the relationship between I and C? As Marx ascertained, for exchange to take place between the sectors, certain defined conditions must be satisfied. The condition of equilibrium is the identity:

$$(1-m_1)\Delta I \equiv m_2 \Delta C$$

This gives us the equation for equilibrium that enables us to calculate ΔC when the remaining variables are known:

$$(1-m_1)\Delta I = m_2 \Delta C,$$

hence,

$$\Delta C = \frac{(1-m_1)}{m_2} \Delta I$$

An increase in the production of investment goods clearly leads to a proportionate increase in consumption. However, the coefficient of proportionality, according to which this growth will occur, depends on m_1 and m_2. This coefficient expresses precisely the effect of investment on consumption on the macro-economic scale that is known as the multiplier effect. The equation related to this, and which shows the influence of investment on national income, is as follows,

$$\Delta Y = \Delta I + \Delta C = (1 + \frac{1-m_1}{1-m_2}) \Delta I$$

At the same time, the above relationships reveal the fundamental structural differences in the functioning of the socialist and the capitalist economies. Under socialism, accumulation and outlays on investment have the purpose of extending the productive base of the economy, with the aim of expanding the production of consumer and investment goods in the future. However, in a capitalist economy, accumulation and investment not only have this function, but simultaneously also condition current production.

If we accept productive capacity in sector II as given, then its utilisation to the full depends on the level of production in sector I, in other words, on the level of investment. There exists an optimal level of investment, I_0, creating such a demand for the means of consumption, that allows the productive capacity of sector II to be fully utilised. When this optimal level of investment is greater than the productive capacity available in sector I, then part of the productive potential in sector II cannot be utilised. This contradiction is a characteristic feature of the capitalist system. Because the inequality $I < I_0$ holds in general, productive capacity in sector II remains partly unused.

In theory, this inconsistency may only be overcome by government intervention aimed at reducing the degree of monopoly. In such circumstances, prices would be reduced, consumption would increase, and productive capacity in sector II would be more fully utilised.

2. But what happens in a socialist economy in which the government controls prices? What is interesting here is the influence that a reduction in investment has on the degree of capacity utilisation in both sectors. In the socialist economy, a tendency appears for the same level of production in sector II to be maintained, through the lowering of prices of articles of consumption. At the same time, attempts will be made to shift part of the production of sector I to the satisfaction of consumption needs – for example, the production of machinery will be replaced by production of consumer durables, more building materials will be directed to the rural sector with the aim of expanding productive capacity in agriculture. Another possible response may be to expand the production of consumer goods with the aim of averting the drop in output in sector I. Obviously, this solution assumes that the prices of articles of consumption are lowered, or wages, and therefore personal incomes, are increased.

In this way, the undesirable multiplier effects on the economy as a whole, that is on national income, employment and capacity utilisation, are avoided, whereas in a capitalist economy these effects are unavoidable. Therefore, that which is a serious problem in the capitalist system does not, in theory, arise in a socialist economy. Consequently, under socialism when investment is reduced, reactions can occur that are the opposite of those that would occur in a capitalist economy: the reduction in investment in a given year will lead not to diminished consumption, but conversely to its increase. Inflexible prices and the multiplier effect are characteristic features of a capitalist economy. However, in a socialist economy, prices are elastic, and the effects go counter to those that are normally associated with the operation of that multiplier. Clearly these are not the main differences between these two socio-economic systems. Undoubtedly, however, they do express very fundamental economic features of each of them.

3. Before passing on to the third question, namely price formation in a socialist economy on the basis of decentralised decision-making by individual enterprises, it is necessary to say a few words about the process of free competition itself. Free competition in the classic form in which it is treated in political economy textbooks never existed in capitalist economies. Even in the nineteenth century it had the character of imperfect competition, because there always appeared various kinds of local monopolies. Twentieth-century capitalism is characterised by competition between particular duopolies and oligopolies.

A socialist economy in which price formation is completely at the discretion of enterprises is an extreme case. However, this may serve as a model in which to discuss problems that arise in circumstances approaching it. In this case, phenomena may appear that are similar to those which arise in a capitalist economy, namely, socialist enterprises may enter into understandings to maintain rigid prices. Cases of imperfect competition, usually attendant upon tendencies towards concentration, may also arise. In these circumstances, the negative results of the multiplier effect may also appear in a socialist economy.

The above reasoning may be criticised on the grounds that it does not take into account the fact that in a socialist economy the threat of insufficient investment does not arise. Nevertheless, the fact remains that, under socialism, the level of investment may be too low relative to the level that is appropriate to the normal possibilities of economic development. It is of course possible to introduce *ex post* controls, consisting of special taxes on the super-normal profits that accrue to enterprises from a monopoly position in the market, or from less than full use of their capacity. However, for this instrument to be effective, the rate of taxation must be made very strictly dependent on the degree of capacity utilisation by the enterprise. Every different method of taxing super-normal profits would contain arbitrary elements and could thereby eliminate the incentive function which profits should fulfil. The one objective criterion therefore remains the degree of utilisation of the fixed capital that the enterprise has at its disposal. However, ascertaining this precisely would require a bureaucratic apparatus that would not be in the least bit smaller than that which is required when prices are fixed by central agencies. Besides, the examination and making of decisions relating to the degree of an enterprise's capacity utilisation by the state authorities would itself already be tantamount to a serious encroachment on the autonomy of the enterprise's production plan.

This is certainly a fundamental issue. There is no doubt that when prices are determined wholly by the enterprise, the inequality $I < I_0$ may occur, that is, a situation in which the level of investment may be lower than the optimal level. For this reason the problem warrants a comprehensive analysis. Nevertheless, it is possible to state in advance that an indispensable condition for ensuring the full use of economic potential is central control of price formation.

I do not wish to idealise this solution. It may be that under this system of price-setting as well enterprises may, despite everything, exploit various opportunities for unjustified price increases and thereby raise their profits. In any case, however, this system keeps the incentive role of profits which will encourage enterprises not to increase prices, but to lower their costs of production and increase its volume.

Finally, a further problem arising out of autonomous price-fixing by enterprises should be pointed out. This is the possibility that unwarranted differences in income between workers in different enterprises may arise, which may cause dissatisfaction. This in particular cannot be a matter of indifference from the point of view of socialist relations in society.

7 Observations on Labour Productivity*

In the current discussion on the subject of raising the productivity of labour, the latter is often treated as a panacea for accelerating economic development and increasing prosperity. In a sense, this brings to mind the debates of a few years ago, in which the use of a system of incentives in economic management was regarded as such a panacea. I took part in that discussion, warning that the matter is not as straightforward as it might at first glance appear.† My observations now are in a similar vein. Undoubtedly the growth of labour productivity is one of the determining factors in economic development. However, the stress that is laid on increasing it in particular branches of production should depend on the nature of that increase on the one hand, and on conditions in the economy as a whole on the other.

I

In considering the effects of an increase in labour productivity, it is necessary first of all to distinguish two sets of circumstances:

1. An increase in labour productivity leading to higher production with a constant level of employment.
2. An increase in labour productivity leading to a decrease in employment at a constant level of employment. If, for example, in some

* First published in *Życie Gospodarcze*, no. 31 1960.

† See the article, included in the present volume, entitled 'Workers' Councils and Central Planning'.

factory the speed of operation of certain machines is increased, then with a given labour force there will follow an increase in production resulting from a more intensive use of the productive equipment and the labour force. If however, the increase in productivity is the result of the same machines, operating at the same speed, and being worked by a smaller number of workers, then the same level of production corresponds to a decrease in employment.

The first case indicates a direct increase in national output. The second case merely indicates the saving of labour power, which may be more or less advantageous for the economy, depending on the situation in the labour market.

II

After making this distinction, it should be noted that the more useful kind of increase in a factory's production, through a better use of its given productive equipment and workforce, may also, in practice, present various complications.

First of all, a necessary condition for such a favourable solution is additional supplies of raw materials. In view of this, it would be necessary to increase production of the appropriate raw materials, and/or expand exports in order to allow for reduced exports of those raw materials, or the increase in imports of them, otherwise the balance of payments would be disturbed. It should be pointed out that such a successful coordination of production (and exports, when it comes to bridging the gap through foreign trade) may not always be possible, and in any case will not occur automatically in the course of achieving the general aim of increasing labour productivity.

If, as a result of a lack of additional raw materials supplies, the goal of increasing production overall is abandoned, and labour productivity is nevertheless forced up, then the first case turns into the second one. I.e., instead of increasing production, a decrease in employment will result. If, for example, the increase in productivity is the result of a faster rate of operation by machines, but materials supply problems render an increase in output impossible, then employment will be reduced to some extent. At the same time, part of the productive apparatus will stand idle, when previously it was active. This will be off-set by the faster operations of the machines when active, with the result that the overall degree of capacity utilisation will stay the same.

III

Problems with expanding production may arise not only on the side of input supplies, but also on the marketing side. Thus, for example, an increase in the production of consumer goods for which there is no market demand leads only to a build-up of stocks. An increase in production in these circumstances would therefore bring no benefit to the economy. On the contrary, it would tie up raw materials and render ineffective the foreign currency spent on achieving it.

Arguing in a systematic manner, it is obviously possible to say that this danger will not arise, since an increase in the commodities available allows for a corresponding increase in real incomes, through an increase in wages or a decrease in prices. But even then, the matter is far from simple. With higher real incomes, there is an increase in demand not only for those consumer goods whose supply happens to be increasing as a result of higher productivity, but also for those (e.g., foodstuffs) whose supply has not increased. This makes increasing incomes more difficult, since in these conditions it leads to disequilibrium in certain markets.

In theory it is possible to get round this by changing relative prices, namely by lowering the prices of the surplus commodities sufficiently in relation to the prices of other consumer goods. To secure equilibrium in all markets, however, it may not be enough merely to lower the prices of the surplus commodities. This is because, as we have already mentioned, the resulting increase in real incomes may cause an increase in demand for other products as well. In this case, a simultaneous increase in the prices of those other commodities is necessary. The increase in real incomes would then arise as a result of the difference between the effect of the reduction in the prices of other consumer goods. If, however, the price increase affects necessities, then this manoeuvre would encounter practical difficulties, since the population may view unfavourably an increase in real incomes achieved in this way. Besides, at low levels, real incomes may actually fall as a result of such a price reform.

If, as a consequence of the above-mentioned difficulties, real incomes are not increased to a level appropriate to the higher production of those consumer goods benefiting from the increased productivity, then obviously there will be an increase in stocks as stated above.

IV

It is obvious that an increase in productivity leading to a better utilisation of productive capacity will contribute to raising production in the economy overall. However, if the additional demand or market does not exist, then difficulties arise for the balance of foreign trade, or in the stockpiling of unsold commodities. But avoiding these undesirable effects leads to the abandonment of increasing production, and therefore to the use of the increase in productivity solely to lower the required level of employment. Let us now examine the circumstances under which this 'saving of labour' brings substantial benefits.

It is clear that if a country suffers from a general shortage of labour, i.e., if the labour force and not the productive apparatus is the bottleneck holding up production, then the raising of labour productivity is indispensable for the full utilisation of that productive capacity. If, however, there is no general labour shortage, then additional labour saving allows working hours to be reduced. If this is not done, then labour saving leads to a reduction in the migration of labour from the rural economy, reduced employment of married women and young workers, and ultimately to unemployment in one form or another. In this case, the increase in labour productivity within factories does not raise the social productivity of labour, since it is offset by the lower level of employment.

This reasoning does not, however, conclude the subject. Although the labour force *as a whole* may be altogether sufficient to man the productive apparatus, *in certain sectors* shortages may occur. Labour shortages may arise in particular branches of production (e.g., in mining), among particular age and sex groups (e.g., there may be a deficit of adult men) and finally in certain regions. In these cases, the application of labour-saving arrangements, appropriate to the particular labour shortage, takes on a fundamental importance, although this does not necessarily warrant the implementation of such a policy on the scale of the economy as a whole.

V

Hitherto we have implicitly assumed that we are dealing with a given productive apparatus, and we have therefore considered the consequences of raising labour productivity in that given economic situation. Let us now imagine that we are drawing up some long-term national economic plan, and that we are considering the influence that an acceleration in labour productivity will have on our development of this plan. An argument conducted along the lines of the one above will here give different results.

In this case, an increase in labour productivity of the kind that leads to improved utilisation of productive equipment (whether existing or new), takes on a different aspect. Essentially, the greater production obtained from a given plant allows the investment required to realise a given programme of production to be reduced, and this saving in investment in its turn allows either a reduced level of investment and a correspondingly higher level of consumption, or the achievement of a greater increase in national output with a given level of investment. In both cases, the problems of supplies and markets, which were mentioned in sections II and III, will be diminished, if not altogether eliminated, since the necessary changes in the structure of production may be obtained to a great extent by the appropriate changes in the structure of investment.

In this context, the modernisation of old factories acquires a special significance. Such modernisation enables their productive equipment and workforces to be better employed, at the cost of relatively small investment outlays.

As for making arrangements for 'pure' labour-saving in a long-term plan, i.e., reducing the level of employment corresponding to a given production plan, the matter may be represented in a similar way to the results of our considerations relating to a current economic situation, that is, under the assumption that the productive capacity is given. The long-term plan anticipates a particular increase in productive capacity which, combined with assumptions about the technology to be used, defines the requirements for labour. To induce labour-savings to a greater degree than is required to obtain such a demand for labour as will be necessary to employ the forecast supply of labour may only be done in order to carry out a reasonable programme of reducing working hours. Moreover, such an induction of labour-savings often requires considerable additional investment outlays.

Obviously we are also concerned here with the demand for labour not only overall, but in particular sectors too. In view of this, efforts to raise productivity must be set out in the plan differently according to the respective branches of industry, sex and age groups, and regions.

VI

In summary, two cases of increasing labour productivity need to be distinguished: (1) When it is linked to better use of productive equipment, and (2) when it constitutes 'pure' labour saving.

With a given productive capacity in the first case, it is possible to increase production holding the level of employment constant. However, this may precipitate problems with the balance of foreign trade, or the stock-piling of unsold goods. If increasing production is renounced, then case (1) becomes case (2). 'Pure' labour saving in a situation where there is no shortage of labour leads only to a reduced rate of employment, which does not raise the *social* productivity of labour.

In the context of planning, where we are dealing with an expansion of the productive apparatus, then case (1) is undoubtedly beneficial, in that the greater production obtained from given productive equipment allows the construction of new capacity to be diminished. At the cost of this saving in investment, consumption may be increased, or a greater increase in national output may be obtained with the same level of investment. In case (2) the acceleration of labour productivity is useful only to prevent shortage of labour in the economy as a whole, or in some specific sector of it, or to carry out a reasonable programme for reducing working hours. But it should be borne in mind that such induced labour savings may themselves often require considerable additional outlays on investment.

It follows from this that labour productivity policy ought to have a distinctly differentiated and composite character, taking into account the nature of the increase in such productivity and its repercussions on the size and structure of national output and the situation in the labour market.

In conclusion it should be added that raising the productivity of labour is often approached from the point of view of reducing costs and increasing financial accumulation. In a socialist economy, these issues can be settled by applying appropriate pay, price and fiscal policies. Policy on labour productivity ought to be subordinated to the carrying out of production goals and balancing the demand and supply of labour, while allowing for a programme of reductions in working hours.

8 On the Basic Principles of Long-term Planning*

I have in mind here the following four principles:
(I) The principle of coordinating the different parts of the plan;
(II) The principle of the efficiency of planned investment;
(III) The principle of plan realism; and
(IV) The principle of maintaining consumption in the near future.
These are rather elementary and well-known principles, so that a reconsideration of them may seem superfluous. However, from time to time it is useful to go back to the basic elements of planning, especially at a time when we are experiencing economic difficulties.[1] Secondly, as we shall see, the principles here discussed are not at all as simple as they may appear, and their application runs counter to many widely held opinions.

I The principle of coordinating the different parts of the plan

The inclusion of this principle into our discussion may appear questionable. The need to balance the plan is obvious, and infringements of this principle, leading to deficits in commodity balances, in the foreign trade account, or the labour market, undermine the realism of the plan. In view of this, are these problems not dealt with under the principle of plan realism? In fact we are here dealing with a more general issue, namely with a methodology of plan construction that will enable us to avoid shortages as well as surpluses.

In constructing the long-term plan, we ought to start off with a certain assumed rate of economic growth. Obviously one can and

* First published in *Życie Gospodarcze*, no. 24 1963.

should consider a few such plan variants, but in each case this growth rate is a parameter that is given. Then we must also accept certain assumptions about the future structure of consumption and the relationship between consumption and non-productive investments.[2] These assumptions already demarcate broadly the division of national income into productive investment, non-productive investment, stock increases and consumption. They also designate to a great extent the structure of national output and productive investment. We say to a great extent and not wholly since the structure of production will also depend (a) on the choice between technologically different ways of achieving a given production effect (e.g., the choice between thermal and hydro-electric power stations); and (b) on the choice of directions of foreign trade (including the decision whether to produce a given commodity at home, or to import it). In both these cases, the choice is made on the basis of an analysis of investment efficiency, which we shall discuss more fully in the second section.

Summing up, we may state that the structure of production determines (a) the rate of growth of national income; (b) the prospective structure of consumption and its relationship to non-productive investment; and (c) the outcome of analyses of alternative methods of production and directions of foreign trade.

In the light of this reasoning, the method of *starting* plan construction by assuming some growth rate for particular sectors of production is manifestly groundless. Essentially, their rate of development determines the rate of growth of national output, which is the sum of the net output of all sectors. In turn, to a particular growth rate of national output, combined with further assumptions about the structure of consumption and its relationship to non-productive investment, corresponds a certain structure of production, defined by that overall growth rate, as well as particular growth rates for the individual sectors of the economy similarly defined. In general, these growth rates will be completely different from the more or less arbitrary initial assumptions.

Inevitably, therefore, there will appear shortages in some branches of production and surpluses in others. The shortages will be eliminated as long as the principle of plan realism, which we shall discuss below, is observed. However, a tendency may appear to maintain high plan targets in the 'surplus' branches of production, especially in those sectors whose rapid development symbolises for many people economic and technological progress, e.g., the energy and the machine tools industries. This approach is wrong because it leads to exaggeration in the plan of the requirements for certain products, or the classification of surpluses of a given product as reserves. Obviously reserves are extremely useful in the plan. But they should be created in sectors whose production targets are threatened (we shall deal with this in our discussion of plan realism), and not in a random way, solely out of a desire to maintain high targets as supposed indicators of progress. In reality, such tolerance of excessive targets leads to waste, whether it be through the over-estimation of requirements already in the plan, or through the creation of unnecessary reserves, which encourage even greater demands for resources, and may contribute to increased requirements in the course of the plan's fulfilment.

Obviously account should be taken of the fact that the growth coefficient for some industry, which may have turned out to be too high with a given rate of growth of national output, will not be at all too high when we examine a plan variant with a higher economic growth rate. Then the domestic demand for the output of that industry increases, and it may also serve to develop exports needed to achieve greater imports (obviously, if this is possible from the point of view of the absorption capacity of markets abroad). But this greater demand will occur in connection with a general change in the development coefficients of individual industries, which coefficients will now be coordinated with a faster rate of growth of national output.

With reference to these considerations, it is worth reflecting on the notion that industrialisation is usually treated as an aim in itself, despite the fact that it is only derived from the successful realisation of a long-term plan of economic development, especially in less developed countries. A growth rate of industrial production that is faster than the rate of growth of agricultural production is the result of the following causes:

(1) With rising standards of living, the consumption of industrial goods rises faster than the consumption of foodstuffs.

(2) In less developed countries, domestically produced articles are substituted for imported industrial products. Only at a later stage do these domestically produced articles become significant in the export trade. This is the result as much of problems with balancing foreign trade while undergoing rapid economic development, as of the requirements for efficiency in such trade.

(3) If the growth of the economy is accelerated, then the share of investment in national income rises. This in turn increases

the share of industry in national output, since agricultural output does not play the significant role in investment that it does in consumption.

In this way, it is not industrialisation that determines the development plan. Rather, industrialisation arises as an inevitable consequence of the requirements of the plan.

Similarly, the rapid growth of machine production ought to be decided by the needs defined in the development plan, and not by slogans about mechanisation. The same factors should determine the development of machine industries as those which warrant the necessity for rapid industrial development, namely (a) the rise in the share of consumer durables in consumption as living standards rise, (b) the substitution of domestically produced machinery for imported equipment, and at a later stage its export, and (c) the rise in the share of productive investment in national income.

II The principle of the efficiency of planned investment

This states that a given increase in national income should be obtained with the smallest possible investment outlay, while maintaining equilibrium in the labour market and in foreign trade.* The smaller the productive investment required to achieve the planned increase in national income, the greater will be that part of the increase which it will be possible to devote to consumption and non-productive investment.

We apply this principle primarily in analysing the capital-intensity of new plant, and the higher labour productivity which rises in line with it. That capital-intensity ought to be such that the productivity of labour in the new factories will enable the labour market to be balanced, after allowing for the programme of shortening working hours. If capital-intensity is too low then, at the assumed rate of growth of national income, a labour shortage will appear. If it is too high, then the labour market will not clear. In the first case the plan cannot be fulfilled. In the second case it is irrational, since it assumes unnecessar-

* We assume here, as before, that a given structure of future consumption is aimed at. Of course there remains the problem of choosing the most efficient structure of consumption, i.e., selecting from the range of equivalent but differently structured variants of consumption that variant which requires the lowest amount of inputs. But this problem, which has not been adequately examined hitherto, is outside the scope of this article.[3]

ily high investment outlays, while at the same time leaving unused labour reserves. The rise in labour productivity, like industrialisation, is not an end in itself, but merely a means of balancing the labour market with a given rate of economic growth. Obviously, the faster is the planned rate of growth, the greater will have to be the effort to raise the productivity of labour.

However, even if the capital intensity of the new plants is not set to achieve unnecessarily high labour productivity, this does not mean that this capital-intensity is optimal. Labour savings may be obtained in various ways, and the variant requiring the lowest investment outlays should be selected. It is no use saving on living labour by expensive automation if the same economy could be obtained by a less costly outlay on, for example, more rudimentary mechanisation of street cleaning. The widespread view that the best devices are those so-called most advanced techniques in the world is erroneous. The calculation of the efficiency of investment should indicate what is best. It is not necessarily the case that what is worthwhile for an American capitalist must be worthwhile for us. Low cost production depends on economising not only on labour, but also on investment outlays.

In connection with this, the importance of modernising existing plants ought to be underlined. This can often secure as much of a saving of labour as an increase in productive capacity, at the cost of relatively small investment inputs.

Let us now examine the question of investment efficiency from the point of view of maintaining a desired balance of trade. Here both investments promoting exports and those reducing imports enter into consideration. The latter in turn are divided up into investments aimed at developing substitutes for imported raw materials, and at economising on raw materials. It should be possible to calculate what is the most efficient way of obtaining the foreign currency to purchase essential imports.

It should further be pointed out that this calculation is not at all an easy task, in view of the difficulties in foreign trade that are encountered with a rapid rate of economic growth. The injunction to concentrate on the most effective export sectors turns out to be impracticable. Here the limited overseas market for certain products (e.g., in the export of machinery), or problems with expanding certain branches of production, even in the long run, due to technical and organisational factors (limited natural resources, shortages of certain types of labour, the necessarily gradual introduction of new methods of production into existing factories, and so on) are obstacles.

In such conditions, effective import-reducing investments, especially those leading to raw material economies and to the production of substitute materials, have a far-reaching importance and become the central issue of the plan. Essentially, problems with balancing foreign trade constitute one of the most serious barriers to the achievement of a high economic growth rate. The need to resort to disadvantageous exports contributes to raising the investment outlays necessary to achieve a given increase in national income. It therefore has a detrimental effect on consumption, as a result of which rapid rates of development become obviously less attractive. Moreover, at a certain rate of economic growth, the balancing of imports with exports may become altogether impossible.

In view of this, labour productivity becomes somewhat dependent on achievements obtained in economising on materials used. The greater are the economies realised, the faster may be the rate of growth. This in turn affects the increased requirements in relation to labour productivity.

The problems of developing agriculture may serve as a typical example here. Of these problems, the main question that emerges is that of animal feedstuffs, which seriously affects the balance of trade. The most effective means of resolving this difficulty is through increasing the use of protein fodder and fertilisation to raise domestic yields. Because of the predominance of light soils in Poland, increasing yields by mechanisation cannot play any substantial role in resolving this difficulty. Mechanisation will primarily effect the saving of labour and increasing agricultural production in those areas where there is a shortage of labour. Thus, mechanisation is necessary in such proportions and of such a kind as to help remove the obstacles to agricultural development. It should be concentrated first of all on those farms affected by labour shortages and on state farms, and it ought to be introduced when disused holdings are taken over by state farms and agricultural co-operatives. But even in those cases, it is not necessary to imitate the example of American farms in mechanisation: it is enough to content ourselves with less labour-saving techniques appropriate to an economy in which a higher proportion of the population than in the United States works in agriculture.

Just as in the economy in general, labour productivity in agriculture is closely linked with the raw materials base. The rapid development of agriculture, based on mastering the fodder production, requires greater labour productivity as well. More intensive production is a prerequisite for mechanisation, since the aim is to maximise productivity per hectare, and not per worker employed. But given the situation in the labour market, the increase in productivity per hectare requires an increase in the productivity of labour as well.

III The principle of plan realism

We have already mentioned this principle in our discussion of plan coordination. We stated then that obviously shortages should not be introduced into commodity balances and foreign trade. However, this statement is by no means unambiguous, since the notion of a shortage is relative. Assuming optimistic (i.e., so-called 'mobilising') targets, plan fulfilment becomes at least uncertain, despite a formally balanced plan. Optimism can appear at various stages: in setting the standards of material requirements, in forecasting the degree of utilisation of existing productive capacity and the construction and gestation periods of new plants, in assessing export possibilities, and finally in the costing of investments. In this last case, a considerable role, alongside the optimism of the planners, is often played by the blandishments of enterprises seeking to show off a given investment in the best possible light, so that, after having 'attached it to the plan', they can revise its costs radically upwards.

It should be pointed out that if the mobilising effect of optimistic targets is not based on realistic steps taken to realise them, e.g., investments leading to economies in materials usage, then it is eminently dubious. Usually such targets mobilise ideas mainly about manipulating product mixes, more or less readily available deterioration in quality and so on.

In this way, a 'tight' plan emerges, i.e., one that is ambitious but risky, if not already wholly unrealistic. If such a plan fails, which can happen, then it usually causes losses; in other words, the outcome is worse than if planning had been more cautious. The realism of a plan depends on setting it out in such a way as to make the risk of non-fulfilment small.

At this point, the issue of reserves emerges. As we have already mentioned, reserves in the form of increased surpluses in commodity balances ought to be found in those sectors that are especially at risk, i.e., those where even with the greatest effort it is impossible to forecast precisely the situation in the future. The best examples here are in those sectors dependent upon forecasts of the future evolution of exports to the capitalist countries. Such exports will, after all, depend on fluctuations in world markets. As for exports to the socialist countries, we are in a better situation here insofar as we enter into long-term trade agreements with them. Such agreements reduce the need for essential reserves, and thereby also allow a faster rate of growth to be distributed and consumed.

However, the existence of reserves should not prevent us from in principle setting the most exact targets that can be calculated in the cases of, for example, commodity balances and investment outlays. Obviously some uncertainty will remain here too, but an effort should be made to limit this uncertainty to the minimum, and, together with it, the reserves required to be set against it.

The following practices are particularly undesirable: after setting a 'heroic' target, a reserve is set up which, at least partly, offsets the 'heroism' required. This merely encourages the obscuring of the plan: a large reserve may, under the circumstances, turn out to be wholly inadequate.

Apart from reserves in the form of surpluses in commodity balances, a fundamental role is played by reserves of resources, such as reserve stocks of fuel and raw materials, foreign currency reserves and so on. For example, fuel stocks should be sufficient to enable the economy to withstand even quite a severe winter. This would not require an excessive financial burden, since the value of such a reserve is not too great. The failure to observe this principle leads to serious economic losses and suffering.

It is desirable that the foreign currency reserve should be sufficiently large, since all kinds of short-term fluctuations are possible in foreign trade (besides long-term changes which ought to be insured against by running up surpluses on the balance of payments). The problem of bad harvests, which we shall refer to again below, leading to the requirement of additional imports enters as a factor, among others, into the calculation here. However, if there is no such foreign currency reserve, then the period of time allowed in which to accumulate one should not be set too short. Too short a period would require either a considerable temporary slowing down of economic growth, or else cause strains in the plan which may result in substantial losses. Until such a reserve is amassed, there is no alternative but to make use of short-term credits, bear losses on the prices of foreign exchange transactions, and so on.

Such types of operation are on the whole insufficient to secure essential imports of grain in the event of very bad harvests. How then can this problem be resolved if there is an inadequate foreign currency reserve? A solution that depends on reducing imports of raw materials obviously rebounds unfavourably on economic activity, and especially on consumption. But, because of contracts already signed, it is difficult to reduce investment imports. It seems worthwhile to consider planning tree-felling in inverse proportion to harvests. In years of bad harvests, felling would be correspondingly greater than average, and the sale of surplus timber abroad would raise the finance for additional grain imports. In years of good harvests, the situation would be reversed, so that over the whole of the long-term plan, felling would not exceed the accepted quotas. Obviously, a detailed consideration of this subject is beyond the scope of this article.

In conclusion, it should be added that the non-fulfilment of an unrealistic plan, in the final result, will affect mainly consumption. This is because there exists a natural tendency to maintain the continuity of investment processes, in order to avoid tying up capital in unfinished projects. However, the losses due to the non-fulfilment of the plan in the consumption sector should not be under-estimated. The demoralisation of the people has not only various consequences for economic activity, but also, and by no means less importantly, has a very bad effect on the consolidation of socialist ideals in social consciousness.

In the next section, we shall deal more closely with the issue of consumption in long-term planning, but under the assumption that the principle of plan realism is observed.

IV The principle of maintaining consumption in the near future

The greater the increase in national income, the greater is the investment required to bring it about. The greater the ratio of this increase to the level of national income, the greater is the share of productive investment in national income. Precisely because of this, and although in the longer term the cumulative effect of higher growth rates has a positive effect on living standards, in the short term that situation is reversed. The faster growth requires a greater portion of current national income to be set aside for investment, and hence has a detrimental effect on consumption.

The setting of the growth rate in the long-term plan is therefore a compromise between consumption in the short and the long terms.

This throws new light on the importance of analyses of investment efficiency. The savings on investment outlays achieved in this way mitigate this dilemma, diminishing the sacrifices that are borne today for the sake of the future.

But the relationship of dependence that has been sketched out here of the share of productive investment in national income on the latter's rate of growth does not exhaust the issue. In addition, certain factors which have already been mentioned influence the increase in investment outlays as economic growth rises. If there are no labour reserves, then the achievement of a faster planned growth rate must be linked up with a planned increase in labour productivity, which in turn requires additional investment outlays. Besides, too rapid a growth rate leads to cumulative difficulties in balancing foreign trade and renders necessary the resort to less effective investments for forcing exports or discouraging imports. In this way, a faster growth rate effects an increase in the share of investment in national income, which in turn affects living standards in the short term.

It is apparent from this how difficult the decision over the economic growth rate is. The harmful consequences for living standards in the near future of a high long-term growth rate must be borne in mind when making this decision. It is precisely this difficulty that is the reason for drawing up unrealistically optimistic plans which constitute, as it were, a flight into the realms of fantasy, away from the arduous dilemma of consumption in the short and the long terms.

Abiding by the principles of plan realism and maintaining consumption in the near future leads to restraint in setting the growth rate, while the avoidance of waste and conscientious analysis of investment efficiency allows this rate to be kept notwithstanding at a relatively high level.

9 Problems in the Theory of Growth of a Socialist Economy*

The growth of investment and national income in a socialist economy

I

From the point of view of the growth rate of producer and consumer goods' production, the most important factor is the growth of investment in relation to national income. The production of producer goods includes the instruments of labour (machines, buildings and so on), and the objects of labour (materials, fuel, and so on). In the majority of cases, the use of the latter will increase less rapidly than the production of finished goods. This is due to technical and organisational improvements. Therefore, as is often argued, when the production of producer goods rises faster than the production of consumer goods, this can only be because the growth of investment is faster than the growth of national income. Essentially, if investment rises at the same rate as national income, while materials production and so on rises at a slower pace, it would be difficult to substantiate the principle of a faster rate of producer, as opposed to consumer, goods. The purpose of these considerations is to examine whether and in what circumstances investment should rise at a faster rate than national income.

* First published in O. Lange (ed.), *Zagadnienia ekonomii politycznej socjalizmu* (Problems of Socialist Political Economy), Warszawa, Książka i Wiedza, 2nd ed., 1959.

II

Let us denote by I the annual outlay on productive investment, i.e., productive investment in fixed capital at constant prices and with no deduction for depreciation. Let Y stand for national income, also in constant prices and without allowing for depreciation. Y therefore includes gross productive investment, increases in stocks, non-productive investment (housing construction, municipal services and so on), the output of the defence industries, and, finally, the consumption of goods in the narrow sense. (For the sake of simplicity, we shall disregard any difference between imports and exports, under the assumption that these are balanced.) Investment, I, together with the increase in working capital, S, make up that portion of national income that is devoted to productive purposes. The rest, C, is consumption in the broad sense. This gives us the equation:

$$Y = I + S + C \tag{1}$$

Let ΔY now stand for the increase in national income during the year under consideration. We shall attempt to determine the relationship between an increase in national income, investment and the level of national income. The productive effect of investment is represented by $(1/m).I$, where m is the investment outlay required under the given technological conditions to obtain a unit increase in national income. In other words, the increment in national income that results from productive investment as such is equal to $(1/m).I$.

These are by no means all the factors affecting the growth of national income. First of all, productive equipment is subject to a continual process of obsolescence and wear and tear, so that existing productive capacity is reduced each year by some fraction which we may define by a. For this reason, national income is reduced in each year by $a.Y$, if there are no offsetting factors in operation. This process reverses the increase in national income that comes about as a result of the realisation of investment outlays.

Finally, there is in addition a tendency for national income to rise as a consequence of improvements that are independent of the process of investment. Increases in output from the existing productive apparatus will be accruing continually thanks to improvements in the organisation of work, economies in the use of raw materials and so on. Because of this, national income will rise in a given year by $u.Y$, where u is the coefficient that represents the influence of these improvements.

Thus we arrive at the following equation for the increase in national income, ΔY, in a given year, as a function of investment, I, and the level of national income, Y, in that year:

$$\Delta Y = \frac{1}{m} . I - a . Y + u . Y \qquad (2)$$

It should be pointed out that, in the above explanation, we have disregarded, for the sake of simplicity, the effect of the gestation period of investment. In reality, the outlay on investments in a given year is not generally equal to the value of the projects completed in that year. However, if we assume a constant mean gestation period, the above simplification does not affect fundamentally the analysis of long-run economic processes which we are here advancing.

Dividing up both sides of equation (2) by national income, Y, we get:

$$\frac{\Delta Y}{Y} = \frac{1}{m} . \frac{I}{Y} - a + u \qquad (3)$$

This formula shows the relationship of dependence between the increase in national income and the share of investment in that income. In other words, given the coefficients m, a, and u, the share of productive investment, I, in national income, Y, determines wholly the rate of growth of national income. The greater is I/Y, the greater is this growth rate.

III

The question now arises whether equation (3) can also be used in the analysis of growth in a capitalist economy. The answer to this question is negative. It is in the interpretation given to the coefficient u that the difference between the capitalist and socialist systems appears.

In a socialist economy, productive capacity is, at least in principle, fully utilised. By means of improvements in the organisation of labour, more economic use of materials and so on, it is nevertheless possible to obtain continual increases in production in relation to fixed capital. If this process progresses at a uniform rate over time, then u remains constant.

By contrast, in a capitalist economy, the degree of utilisation of the productive apparatus is continually fluctuating, and may even be subject to long-term changes. Coefficient u will here express primarily relative changes in national income due to changes in capacity utilisation. Over the course of business cycles, coefficient u is not only variable, but even changes its sign from plus to minus and vice versa.

In a capitalist economy, the degree of capacity utilisation depends on the relationship between demand and the size of productive potential. Because of this, u is not an independent coefficient, but reflects varying degrees of success in marketing the output of existing productive capacity. It is only in a socialist economy, in which planning secures the permanent full employment of productive potential, that coefficient u comes to represent solely the effect of organisational and technical improvements that do not require investment outlays.

IV

Before we start our analysis of investment and national income growth using equation (3), let us consider the other components of national income, i.e., the increase in stocks, S, and consumption, C, in the broad sense.

As far as stocks are concerned, we may presume that they increase *pari passu* with national income; i.e., that the rise in working capital is proportional to the increment in national income, ΔY:

$$S = n . \Delta Y \qquad (4)$$

Combining this with equation (1), we get the following equation for consumption, C:

$$C = Y - I - n . \Delta Y \qquad (5)$$

Dividing this equation by Y, we get:

$$\frac{C}{Y} = 1 - \frac{I}{Y} - n . \Delta Y \qquad (6)$$

The share of consumption in national income is therefore smaller the larger are the share of investment and the rate of growth of national income. Given coefficients m, a, and u, the rate of growth of national income increases as the share of investment in national income rises. In such conditions, the function expressed in equation (6) reduces itself to a direct and indirect fall in the share of consumption in national income as the share of investment rises.

V

For the time being we shall discuss the particular case in which coefficients m, a, and u remain constant. Later on we shall consider the effects of possible changes in m, that is the investment outlay needed to obtain a unit increase in national income, allowing for technical progress. As we shall see then, technical progress need not necessarily preclude the possibility of m staying constant: technical progress undoubtedly increases the capital outlay per worker, but not necessarily per unit of output.

Assuming that m, a, and u are constant, then it is immediately apparent from equation (3) that, if the share of investment in national income, I/Y, stays constant too, then the relative growth of national income, $\Delta Y/Y$, remains fixed as well. But obviously the invariability of I/Y means that investment is rising *pari passu* with national income. Therefore we can say that the growth of investment at the same rate as that of national income provides for a uniform growth of national income. In other words, in order to obtain expanded reproduction at a constant rate, it is not necessary for investment to rise faster than national income.

It is now easy to show that, with a constant rate of growth of national income, consumption also rises in the same proportion as investment. This follows directly from equation (6): if I/Y and $\Delta Y/Y$ are constant, then there is no change in C/Y. Hence consumption rises in the same proportion as national income.

From equation (3) it also follows that, as has already been indicated, the rate of growth of national income will be faster, the greater is the share of investment in national income, with a given m. Does this mean that the state can regulate at will the growth rate of national income, by determining the share of investment in that income? First of all, at a very fast rate of economic growth the share of consumption in national income would be small, and therefore the level of consumption in the short run would also be low, which is obviously undesirable.

Furthermore, in seeking to carry out the decision to raise the growth rate, an obstacle in the form of a labour shortage would be met. Let us suppose that national income and investment are rising at a rate of 8% per annum, as an example. As a result of technical progress, the amount of labour required to man the productive equipment that is entered into production in a given year will not rise by 8%, like its productive capacity, but, say, by 3%, because labour productivity is rising by 5%. If, under these circumstances, the labour market remains in equilibrium, then increasing the rate of growth of investment and national income to 9% will turn out to be futile. Essentially, labour productivity is increasing still at an annual rate of 5%, whereas the demand for labour, as a result of the manning requirements of new equipment, is rising by 4%. Consequently, this new equipment cannot be fully utilised.

Obviously the balance in the labour market will limit the rate of economic growth only as long as m is fixed. Intensive mechanisation can indeed help to overcome a shortage of labour, but this can only happen at the cost of additional investment, in which case m will rise. The shortage of labour does not altogether prevent the growth rate of national income from being accelerated. But it means that the share of investment in national income, I/Y, which is necessary to obtain this faster growth rate is greater. As a result, a fall in the share of consumption will be more widely experienced as the limit of the labour force is reached. Thus consumption in the short term will then be correspondingly lower. In this way the shortage of labour will still have a restraining influence on the effectiveness of the decision to accelerate the rate of economic growth.

Irrespectively of these general reasons, the acceleration of the growth rate may turn out to be unrealisable because of the existence of bottlenecks in the economy. The causes of such bottlenecks may be primarily organisational difficulties that emerge with the rapid development of particular sectors of the economy. Here one of the fundamental factors may be the long construction period for investment projects in a given industry. This necessitates the construction of many projects at once in order to achieve higher production growth. Different kinds of organisational problems may occur in different sectors with their own peculiar characteristics, e.g., in agriculture.

Faster economic growth may also be constrained by difficulties in foreign trade. The growth of national income requires continually increasing imports, especially of raw materials and semi-fabricates. This situation demands an appropriate expansion of exports, which may prove difficult. These difficulties will obviously be greater the faster is the rate of growth of national income, and hence also the growth rate of imports. Overcoming these problems by inducing more rapid production of readily exportable commodities may require considerable investment outlays. The effect of this will be to increase m, as we saw in the case of a labour shortage. Organisational difficulties in specific sectors of the economy may prove to be even more serious obstacles to such a strategy.

VI

What will happen if investment rises more rapidly than national income? The share of investment in national income will then increase of course. If we continue to hold our assumption of constant m, a, and u, then it means that the rate of growth of national income will accelerate. However, will it be possible to achieve faster growth if the limiting factors discussed above become effective? If we consider only the problem of balancing the supply and demand for labour, then it is immediately apparent that, with a constant m, the growth of national income may only be accelerated if there are reserves of labour available. If there are not, then a faster rate of economic growth will require increasing mechanisation, and thus m will have to rise. As a result, in the case of the economy with a constant m which we are now examining, a rise in the growth rate of national income may only be obtained if the labour force is reinforced from existing reserves. The exhaustion of these reserves will gradually check the rate of economic growth, which will eventually settle down at a level appropriate to the current balance in the labour market.

It is apparent from equation (6) that the rising share of investment, I/Y, and the rise in working capital, $n.Y/y$, in national income, will involve a fall in the share of consumption. This will lead to a slowing down in the growth of consumption, at least at the start of the period. In the long run, however, consumption will undoubtedly be higher than it would have been, had the rate of growth of national income not been temporarily accelerated. We can show this with an example covering a six-year period, in which the growth rate in each year is as follows:

Year	I	II	III	IV	V	VI
Growth rate (%)	8	9	10	10	9	8

In year I, the rate of growth is 'normal' and comes to 8%. It accelerates in years II and III, and then slows down in year V and VI. In year VI it returns to its normal level of 8%. The share of consumption in national income falls in years II and III, and rises in years V and VI, returning in year VI to its level of year I. Since national income rises from year I to year VI at an average annual rate of 9%, and the share of consumption is the same in year VI as in year I, then consumption also rises over the whole period at an average rate of around 9% per annum. Its growth is therefore greater than it would have been if the growth rate of the economy had not been accelerated, but had risen at an annual rate of 8% throughout.

Summing up, a rate of growth of investment that is faster than that of national income leads to a faster rate of economic growth. This strategy is feasible provided that some reserve of labour is available. But after it has been exhausted, the rate of growth is bound to fall back to a level appropriate to the current balance in the labour market. Increasing the share of investment and working capital in national income slows down the growth of consumption, at least at the start of the period of accelerated economic growth. However, in the longer run, consumption benefits from this acceleration in the growth of national income.

It should be added that even before labour reserves have been exhausted, the acceleration in economic growth may be curbed by the emergence of bottlenecks in particular sectors of the economy. As we have already indicated, this factor may limit the rate of growth of national income regardless of the overall balance in the labour market.

VII

Up until now we have been assuming that coefficients m, a, u, and n remain constant. However, does not the very nature of technical progress imply a continually rising m, i.e., increasing capital outlay in relation to output? We have mentioned already that the tendency to raise capital outlays in relation to employment, or a tendency for stored-up labour to rise in relation to living labour, is inherent in the nature of technical progress. The ratio of output to employment rises as well. But the ratio of capital outlay to production itself depends on the type of technical progress. Since this issue is of fundamental importance, we shall deal with it more extensively.

Let us suppose that there are two workers working on two machines. As a result of technical progress, these two machines are replaced by one which, operated by one worker only, can produce as much as both produced before. Output per worker is thus doubled. The cost of the new machine is certainly greater than that of one of the two machines previously used, so that the capital outlay per worker has also risen. But is it inevitable that the new machine should cost more than the two machines previously in use? Has the capital outlay per unit of output also risen? This cannot be decided a priori. It depends on the type of technical progress that has taken place. If, for example, an innovation consists solely of substituting human labour by machines without increasing production, then the capital outlay has undoubtedly risen in relation to production. But when automation not only replaces workers, but also accelerates the production process, capital outlay relative to output may actually fall.

What kind of technical progress predominates at present? To illustrate this, let us examine changes in the relationship of fixed capital to output in the USSR and in the United States. However, it is not easy, as we shall see, to come to any final conclusion on the basis of the statistics available.

In the Soviet Union, fixed capital doubled between 1940 and 1954, while national income rose 2½ times.* We cannot, however, draw any conclusion from this about the capital-saving nature of technical progress, since during this period there were undoubtedly improvements made in the use of this productive equipment. The effect of these improvements was to increase production relative to capital employed – progress due to such improvements is represented in our basic equation by the coefficient u. But we can perhaps venture a tentative conclusion that technical progress in this period in fact did not involve any significant increase in capital outlay per unit of output.

Figures for the United States are given in the table on p. 79. As we can see, the ratio of fixed capital to production in the US economy as a whole declined over the period from 1929 to 1953 by 25%. But here too it is difficult to attribute this to technical progress, since the possibility of changes in capacity utilisation should be taken into account. Capacity utilisation in 1953 may not be significantly different to that in 1929, since both years were at the peak of their respective business cycles. Nevertheless, more intensive use of labour, which was only partially offset by shorter working hours, undoubtedly contributed to the rise in production relative to capital. In view of this, it is difficult to state here also what was the effect of technical progress itself on the capital–output ratio. Probably it did not contribute to increasing this ratio significantly.

But this still does not give a full picture of the changes that took place in the US economy. It turns out that the fall in the ratio of fixed capital to output came about solely on account of changes in capital investment

* Figures given in A. Notkin, 'Tekhnicheskii progress rost proizvodstva sredstv proizvodstva', *Voprosy Ekonomiki*, no. 12 1955 p. 33.

The ratio of fixed capital to output for production in all sectors of the US economy

	Buildings	Machinery	Total
1929	1.3	0.7	2.0
1953	0.8	0.7	1.5

Source: *Economic Report of the President*, January 1954, p. 60.

in the form of buildings. The value of machinery and equipment in relation to output did not undergo any substantial change. In view of the more intensive use of labour that took place, it would appear that technical progress embodied in machinery and equipment contributed rather to a tendency for capital outlays per unit of output to rise. But in the case of buildings, the situation was reversed.

In further discussion we shall make no assumptions about the prevailing kind of technical progress. We shall merely distinguish between three possible types of technical progress. If capital outlays per unit of output rise, then we shall call this kind of technical progress *capital-intensive*. If the capital–output ratio stays the same, we shall call this progress *neutral*, and if the ratio falls, we shall call it *capital-saving* technical progress. If, in the technical progress proceeding in the economy, the *capital-intensive* kind prevails, then m will rise. If *capital-saving* prevails, then m will fall, while if neither of them predominates, then m remains constant.

VIII

Let us now consider the case where m is continually rising, as a result of the preponderance of capital-intensive technical progress. It then follows from equation (3) that, to maintain a steady rate of growth of national income, it is necessary for investment to rise faster than national income, in order to offset the effect of the rising m. It is easy to see from equation (6) that the share of consumption in national income will fall. In fact, the share of investment in income, I/Y, will rise, while the share of the increase in stocks will stay the same, since the rate of growth of national income is constant.

We are here dealing with linear growth in national income associated with a faster rate of growth of investment, due to the capital-intensive nature of technical progress. In contrast to the case of accelerated economic growth, this process will not come upon the labour force constraint, since the productive capacity of the new plants opened in each year rises steadily at a rate of, say, 8% per annum. Labour productivity is also rising continually at a rate of, say, 5% each year. Thus the demand for labour to man the new plants does not accelerate, but, in our example, continues to rise at an annual rate of 3%.

However, it turns out that even in this case, where *m* is rising without restriction, the process of expanding investment at a faster rate than that of national income cannot be maintained indefinitely. For then the ratio of investment to national income would also rise unrestrained. As we can see from equation (6), a situation would eventually arise in which, as a result of the faster growth of investment, the share of consumption in national income would approach zero, which is obviously absurd.

How can this paradox be explained? We can always stabilise *m*, i.e., the average investment outlay per unit of output, by drawing up an appropriate investment plan. But if capital-intensive technical progress prevails, as in the case we are dealing with here, then this will mean a lower rate of growth of labour productivity. If we were to continue to induce national income growth at an unchanged rate, while stabilising *m*, we would then face a labour constraint.

For example, if with a continually rising *m*, the productive capacity of new plants rises at a rate of 8% per annum, but their productivity rises at a rate of 5% per annum, then, after stabilising *m*, productivity will only rise by, say, 2%. Thus with the same growth rate of the labour force as before (3%), national income cannot rise at the same rate as it did previously.

Holding back the growth of *m* therefore leads to a slowing down in the rate of growth of national income. It is easy to see that this will be associated with a certain decrease in the share of productive investment in national income, I/Y, in relation to its share at the moment when *m* is stabilised. In fact, if the economic growth rate, $\Delta Y/Y$, is to fall, while keeping *m* constant, then, according to equation (3), I/Y should fall.

It is clear that there is no sense in letting *m* rise without limit, and with it the share of investment in national income. Yet it is easy to show that, with capital-intensive technical progress, the rise in *m* may, at a certain period, contribute to increased consumption in the long run if, after that period, *m* is stabilised. This is a problem that is somewhat similar to the one discussed above of temporarily accelerated economic growth.

Let us turn to our next example. At the start of the period under consideration let *m* equal 3, and let us assume that coefficient *a* in equation (2) is equal to coefficient *u*. In this particular case, the equation will appear as follows:

$$\frac{\Delta Y}{Y}=\frac{1}{3}\cdot\frac{I}{Y}$$

We shall examine two variants. In the first, *m* will remain constant. The rate of growth will then come to just 6% per annum, according to the above equation, and with a share of investment in national income amounting to 18%.

In the second case, *m* rises throughout a five-year period, eventually reaching a level of 3.3% National income rises in this case by 8% annually. According to the above equation the share of investment in national income amounts to 24% at the start of the period. At the end of it, the share of investment should be calculated from the equation

$$\frac{\Delta Y}{Y}=\frac{1}{3.3}\cdot\frac{I}{Y}$$

since *m* has now risen to 3.3. In this way, the share of investment in national income, with a growth rate of 8%, can be calculated at around 26%. If at this stage *m* is stabilised, then the rate of growth of national income will drop from 8% to its level in the first variant, i.e., to 6%. The fall in the rate of growth of national income will be the result of a fall in the share of investment in that income from 26% to 20% – this share is higher than it was in the first variant, where it amounted to 18%, because *m* has now risen from 3 to 3.3. These two variants are summarised in the table on p. 82.

In the second variant, over a five-year period, national income will grow at a rate that is about 10% faster than that in the first variant. We assume the share of consumption, *C*, in national income in the first variant to be 80% (allowing 2% for the share of the increase of working capital in national income). In view of this, in the period after the five-year period, when *m* will be stabilised, this share will amount to 78%. As a result, the level of consumption after the five year period will be 8% higher in the second variant, national income will be around 10% higher, and the share of consumption will be approximately 2% less.

We can therefore see that by giving way for a while to a tendency towards capital-intensive technical progress, it is possible to achieve a

% throughout	Variant I ($m = 3$)	Variant II (m rises to 3.3) Start of period	End of period	Period of stable m
Rate of growth of national income	6	8	8	6
Share of investment in national income	18	24	26	20

higher level of consumption in the longer run.* Nevertheless, it can be demonstrated that, in the case under consideration, consumption evolves less favourably in the second variant than in the first. This is an example of how a higher level of consumption in the long run may be achieved at the cost of a slower rate of its expansion in the short run.

IX

We have examined the influence of a predominantly capital-intensive kind of technical progress on the growth of investment and national income. As we have already noted, this is not the only possible kind of technical progress. At a given stage of technical development, innovations of a more *capital-saving* kind may prevail, or indeed none of these types may predominate. In such a situation there will obviously be no need to expand investment at a faster rate than national income in order to secure a constant rate of economic growth at the maximum pace that is consistent with the balance in the labour market. But even if *capital-intensive* innovation were to prevail, then a more rapid growth of investment relative to national income could not be sustained indefinitely. After a certain period, it would become necessary to reduce the capital-intensity of the plan, albeit at the cost of a slower rate of economic growth. The length of this period of faster investment growth will depend on the evaluation of the choice between the growth of consumption in the short term, or in the long run.

It is not possible to deduce from the above reasoning a general rule for deciding on investment and national income growth. The decision as to whether investment should rise at the same rate as, or faster than,

* However, this only holds if m does not rise too fast. If, in the above example, m were to rise not by 10% but by, say, 40%, then consumption in the long run would be the same in both variants. Were m to rise even faster than 40% per year throughout the five-year period, then consumption in the long run would be lower in the second variant than in the first.

national income depends on such factors as the existence of labour reserves and the prevailing type of technical progress, and whether the highest possible level of consumption in the near future is preferred to its maximisation in the long term.

The factors determining the growth rate of national income in a socialist economy

I

The discussion around the growth rate of national income is often reduced to considering the problem of the so-called burden of investment. The faster is the growth rate of the economy, the greater must be the share of productive investment in national income, and hence the smaller will be the share of consumption and non-productive investment. This means that with a rapid economic growth rate, consumption and non-productive investment will grow relatively slowly in the short run. However, in the longer term, the increase in national income would more than compensate for the relatively small share of consumption in national income. Indeed, the outcome for consumption would be even more advantageous the longer the period taken into consideration. In other words, sacrifices in the form of reduced consumption in the short run would facilitate the achievement of a substantially higher level of consumption in the long run. The discussion concentrates on how far it is possible to go in sacrificing the present for the future.

In this kind of analysis it is usual to abstract away from the issues of the balance in the labour market and the foreign trade balance. Yet it is when the rate of growth of national income is accelerated that there may occur both shortages of labour and difficulties in balancing rising imports by a corresponding increase in exports. Overcoming these difficulties by means of intensive mechanisation, partial autarchy, or forcing unprofitable exports abroad, will require enhanced investment outlays. In this case, the acceleration of growth may be achieved solely through increasing the share of productive investment in national income. The sacrifice of consumption in the near future for the sake of consumption in the long term becomes onerous, and this obviously would discourage a decision to increase the economic growth rate.

However, this is not the end of the matter. Even expanding investment outlays may turn out to be ineffective in speeding up the growth of national income beyond a certain level. This is because of the technical and organisational difficulties that arise when particular sectors of the economy are rapidly developed. One of the fundamental causes of such difficulties may be the long construction period of industrial plant of a certain kind. As a result, in order to achieve a rapid rate of growth of production, it becomes necessary to construct many projects simultaneously. Other kinds of organisational problems may appear in sectors that have their own peculiar characteristics, e.g., in agriculture. These bottlenecks in particular sectors of the economy make it impossible to balance foreign trade even with the greatest possible investment effort, if the rate of growth of national income is too fast. Because of this, a decision on the economic growth rate, made on the basis of a tolerable 'sacrifice of the present for the future', may turn out to be simply unrealisable. I shall try to present this problem in a more detailed and rigorous way.

II

In the discussion that follows we shall employ the equations which were used in the first section of this paper, namely

$$\Delta Y = \frac{1}{m}.I - a.Y + u.Y \tag{2}$$

and

$$\frac{\Delta Y}{Y} = \frac{1}{m}.\frac{I}{Y} - a + u \tag{3}$$

where Y is the level of national income in a given year at constant prices; ΔY is the increase in national income during that year; I is gross investment in that year, also at constant prices; m is the investment outlay necessary under the given technical conditions to obtain a unit increase in national income; a is the coefficient of depreciation of productive capacity as a result of ageing and wear and tear of productive equipment; finally, u is the coefficient of national income growth that is due to improvements that are independent of investment, such as better work organisation, steadily increasing economies in raw materials usage, and so on.

In this discussion, we shall assume that the coefficients m, a and u stay constant. This implies, according to equation (3), that the share of productive investment, I, in national income sets the rate of growth of that income. If we increase I/Y by an amount α, then the rate of growth of national income will rise by α/m. Because of this, in the near future consumption will turn out to be less, but, in the longer term, the acceleration of the growth rate of the economy will have such an effect on the level of national income, Y, that the diminished share of consumption will be more than compensated for. Indeed, consumption will turn out to be even greater the longer is the period taken into consideration. Obviously, these benefits in the long term will be smaller the greater is the value of m. This is because the increase in the rate of growth, α/m, will be correspondingly smaller, reflecting the given increase in the burden of investment, I/Y.

The authorities in a socialist country, comparing the disadvantages of relatively lower consumption in the immediate period with the advantages of higher consumption in the longer term, will decide on a particular rate of growth that they will consider to be optimal. Let us call this growth rate r_{opt}. From the above it follows that the greater m is, the smaller will be the future advantages in terms of greater consumption then, in relation to the disadvantages of comparatively lower consumption now, when I/Y is increased. Therefore the optimal level of I/Y will be smaller the greater m is. The same applies *a fortiori* to the optimal growth rate of national income since, according to equation (3), that growth rate is a function of $(1/m).(I/Y)$. We can thus write:

$$r_{opt}=f(m) \tag{7}$$

where f is an inverse function.

III

Up to now we have abstracted away from the problems that may arise in two areas when the growth rate of national income is increased, i.e., where (1) the growth in the supply of labour turns out to be too slow in relation to demand, assuming that there is no policy of rapid induced mechanisation, and (2) the faster is the growth of national income, the faster too will be the growth of essential imports, especially raw materials and semi-fabricates, and balancing this with a suitable programme of export development may turn out to be increasingly difficult. In order to overcome these foreign trade difficulties, partial autarchy may need to be introduced, together with the forcing of exports onto unprofitable markets, or the export of less profitable articles.

These measures, as well as intensive mechanisation, will require increased investment outlays in order to achieve a given increase in national income. In other words, the faster rate of growth of national income will then be obtained with a greater coefficient m. According to equation (7), this increase in m will have a negative effect on the optimal rate of growth r_{opt}.

In fact, let us suppose that the government authorities are examining a range of growth rate variants. Let us put down the coefficient m in the lowest growth variant as m_1. The optimal growth rate will then be:

$$r_{opt} = f(m_1)$$

In reality, m is higher in the other variants. Therefore there will be some other optimal rate of growth set at some level

$$r'_{opt} = f(m_2)$$

where $m_2 > m_1$. Because $f(m_2) > f(m_1)$,

$$r'_{opt} < r_{opt}$$

In other words, the optimal rate of growth is slower here in this second case than it was in the previous one, in which the rapid expansion of the economy did not come up against the limits of the labour market and foreign trade. Thus, in variants with faster growth rates, m was the same as in variants with slower growth rates.

The above argument can be illustrated and made more precise using a graphical presentation (see Fig. 1 below). The graph has m placed on the abscissa. A downward-sloping curve, AB, represents the function $f(m)$. The optimal rate of growth without exogenous limits, r_{opt}, is on the vertical axis opposite the point P on that curve, whose horizontal equivalent is m_1. The different variants of the growth rate are ordered on the vertical axis. The rising curve, CD, represents the magnitudes of m that correspond to each of the variants, and is greater the faster is the rate of growth. Point P' on the intersection of AB and CD shows the optimal rate of growth r'_{opt} that takes into account the limits to growth. In fact, because P' is on the curve AB, we have $r'_{opt} = f(m_2)$, where m_2 is the point on the horizontal axis opposite P'. Furthermore, since P' lies on the curve CD, its equivalent point on the horizontal axis is that m which corresponds to our rate of growth r'_{opt}.

From the graph, it is immediately apparent that $r'_{opt} < r_{opt}$. This difference will be greater the more the curve CD diverges form the vertical line CP. It is this divergence from the vertical that represents

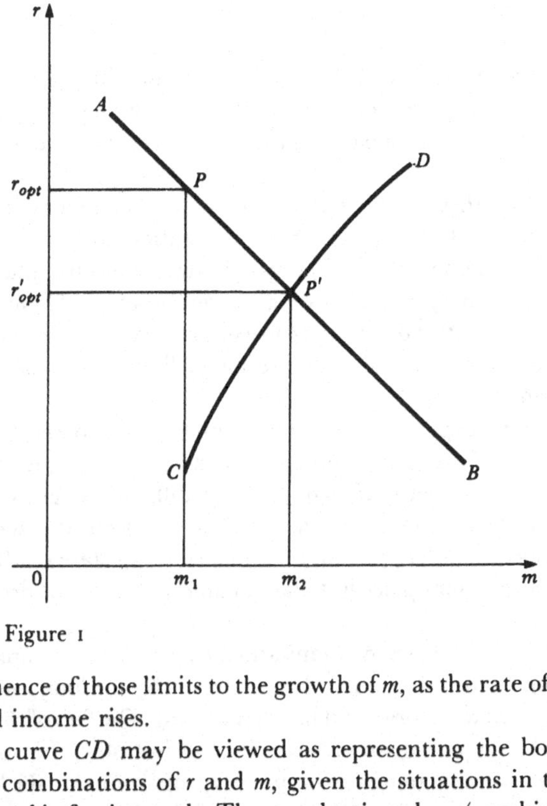

Figure 1

the influence of those limits to the growth of *m*, as the rate of growth of national income rises.

[The curve *CD* may be viewed as representing the boundary of feasible combinations of *r* and *m*, given the situations in the labour market and in foreign trade. Thus production plans (combinations of *r* and *m*) that lie to the right of *CD* would be regarded as excessively capital-intensive, in that they would leave labour reserves unused – i.e., *m* would be too high, and *r* too low, to employ the labour force fully. To the left of *CD* are combinations of *r* and *m* which are infeasible because the rate of growth postulated would be too high at the proposed level of *m* – i.e., there would not be enough labour and foreign trade reserves to allow for an excessively low *m*.

AB represents the policy-makers' choice of the share of investment in the near future. Thus a certain amount of investment resources may be applied to a range of production plans to achieve either a high growth rate, with low capital-intensity in new plants at *A*, or a lower growth rate with higher capital-intensity at *B*, or some combination in between, such as *P* or *P'*. *Translator's note*]

IV

Let us now move onto the third stage of our inquiry in this section, that is to the question of bottlenecks in the development of particular branches of industry which can impede the development of the whole economy.

In their turn, these bottlenecks depend on various kinds of technical and organisational factors. The most straightforward case is that of limited natural resources. For example, in the perspective plan for the Polish economy in 1961–75, known geological reserves of lignite do not allow the rate of extraction in 1975 to exceed a certain level. Similarly, the need for forestry conservation seriously limits the possibilities of felling during the period 1961–75.

Furthermore, experience in carrying out economic plans shows that the expansion of particular industries at a pace that goes beyond a certain rate meets with insurmountable difficulties, even if those carrying out the investment programme have entirely adequate funds at their disposal. Indeed, a phrase to describe this state of affairs has even become commonplace in Poland, namely 'It can't be done!' (*tego nie przerobią*).

Among the technical and organisational factors constraining expansion, an important role is undoubtedly played by the long time that it takes to build new factories and industrial plant. The fact of the matter is that, with a given rate of investment in an industry, the number of plants under construction in an industry is proportional to the length of their construction period. Where this period is long, and the rate of investment is rapid, the number of construction sites becomes so great that the existing technical and management personnel are insufficient to service them properly. As a result, the period of construction is extended. Because of the excessive number of construction sites, capital starts to be tied up in construction rather than contributing to a more rapid development of that industry. It should be noted here that the technical and managerial staff necessary to supervise the construction of new plant should have exceptionally high qualifications; indeed, much higher than those required of the personnel who will eventually manage that plant when it is completed.

Perhaps the best example of how a long construction period can hamper the development of a particular industry is coal-mining in the 1961–75 Polish perspective plan. Despite the assumption of an expansion in this industry of only 30% over the 15 year period, the plan is nevertheless fairly 'tight', since it will be necessary to open up a relatively large number of mines, and it takes eight to ten years to excavate a new pit.

Limited natural resources and long construction periods are not the only technical and organisational influences limiting the rate of development of particular sectors of the economy. Other factors that must be reckoned with are problems of recruiting labour to particular trades, for example again in coal-mining. Another factor is the time that it takes to master new technologies.

The situation is quite different in agriculture, where there is always a certain element of unpredictability. The introduction of higher technologies especially requires a longer time in this sector. The difficulties of achieving greater yields through the application of artificial fertilisers illustrate well the problems of developing production. Let us suppose that we are anticipating the supply to the rural sector of the quantity of fertilisers necessary to obtain the intended harvest. However, the question arises whether farmers will buy these fertilisers. Obviously, they can be 'forced' onto the market by a significant reduction in prices. But when fertilisers become very cheap, it is impossible to be sure that farmers will use them with sufficient care and therefore that the planned crop will indeed be obtained. Thus it transpires that improving the agro-technical qualifications of farmers is indispensable for the development of agricultural production.

V

The emergence of bottlenecks in particular sectors limits the development of the economy as a whole. If, with a given rate of growth of national income, particular industries are set tasks which are beyond them, then the only way out is to increase imports, or diminish exports of the appropriate products. However, this leads to a breakdown in the balance of trade, which may not always be amenable to restoration through cutting imports, or increasing exports through a drive to accelerate expansion in other sectors of the economy which have not yet reached bottlenecks in their development. Thus, all the sectors which turn out domestic substitutes for imports may have already reached bottlenecks in their development. As for exports, there may be difficulties in selling to markets abroad the additional production that can be mobilised. In such a situation, even a considerable increase in investment outlays may not be sufficient to overcome bottlenecks. A rate of growth will then have to be accepted that is lower than the one that could have been achieved had bottlenecks not appeared in particular sectors of the economy.

An example here may be the problems that were revealed in drawing up the perspective plan for the Polish economy in 1961–75. In this plan, the possibilities of increasing the rate of growth of national income were limited by technical and organisational bottlenecks in the development of coal-mining, the steel and non-ferrous metals industries, the chemicals industry, and crop production in agriculture. In fact, bottlenecks in the development of the chemicals industry made it impossible to economize further on imports by substituting synthetic for natural raw materials. The attempt to eliminate grain imports was also unsuccessful because of the impossibility of securing a more rapid increase in grain harvests, due to technical and organisational factors. On the export side, bottlenecks effectively checked the export of coal, steel and chemicals. Because of this, the only remaining possibility was to force through the export of machinery (together with transport equipment and consumer durables), and animal products. In both cases, however, it was important not to go too far because of the considerable risk of problems in supplying markets abroad. (Moreover, in the case of animal products, their export development would depend on imported feedstuffs, which would have limited possible price competitiveness in these markets.) In this way, development bottlenecks in particular sectors of production caused problems in balancing foreign trade when the growth rate of national income exceeded a certain level.

Moreover, it should be noted that even when difficulties in balancing foreign trade can be overcome, despite the emergence of bottlenecks in particular sectors of the economy, this requires additional investment outlays. Therefore, even if it could be done, it would tend effectively to reduce the growth rate of national income (see section II above).

We can now set about summing up our analysis. In the third section above, we showed that the emergence of constraints resulting from labour shortages and difficulties in balancing foreign trade leads to a decline in the rate of growth of national income. In other words, the optimal rate of growth, allowing for the constraints that have been encountered, r'_{opt}, is lower than the optimal rate of growth r_{opt} that the policy-makers in a socialist economy would have selected if these constraints had not arisen. Technical and organisational bottlenecks in the development of particular industries may lead to a further decline in the growth rate. In other words, if in addition the effects of technical

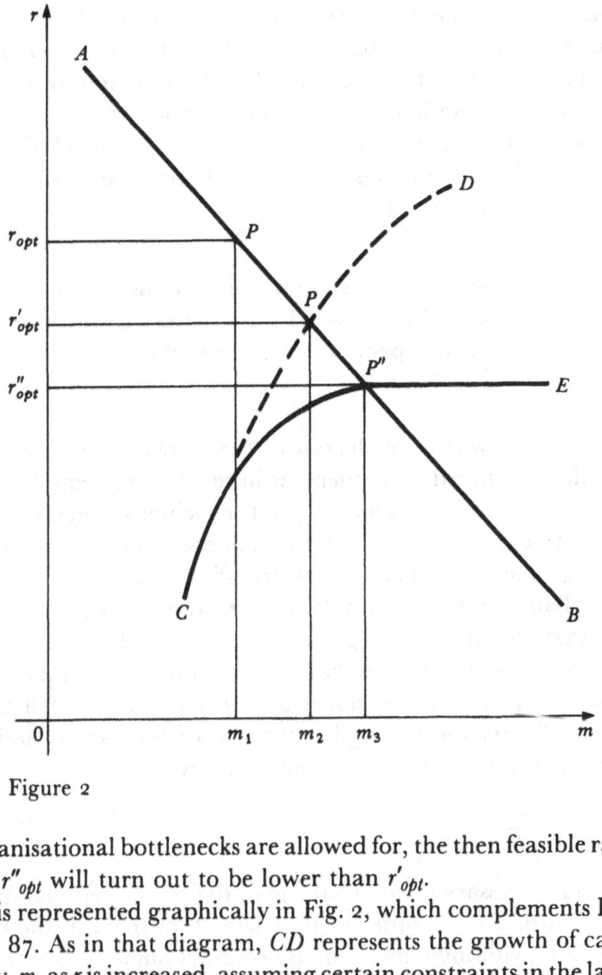

Figure 2

and organisational bottlenecks are allowed for, the then feasible rate of growth r''_{opt} will turn out to be lower than r'_{opt}.

This is represented graphically in Fig. 2, which complements Fig. 1 on page 87. As in that diagram, *CD* represents the growth of capital intensity, *m*, as *r* is increased, assuming certain constraints in the labour market and in foreign trade, but without allowing for bottlenecks in the expansion of particular industries. The curve *CE* takes into account these bottlenecks. The fact that *CE* eventually becomes horizontal indicates that the rate of growth of national income, *r*, cannot exceed a certain maximum because of the incidence of these bottlenecks. In the case illustrated in the diagram, r''_{opt} is equal to that maximum.

The outcome of this analysis is that, in practice, the rate of growth of national income may depend not so much on a comparison between the disadvantages of a lower rate of consumption in the near future and the advantages of a high level of consumption in the long term, but on the technical and organisational factors limiting the development of particular sectors of the economy. Within limitations of this kind, a substantial acceleration of the rate of economic growth may only be obtained by technological innovation in those sectors of the economy affected by those limitations. Such innovation would then enable them to be expanded more rapidly.

The influence of reductions in construction periods and capital intensity in particular sectors on growth prospects in the economy

I

As we have shown above, the rate of growth of national income is to a great degree limited by bottlenecks in the development of particular sectors of the economy, which depend on technical and organisational factors. In particular, one of the most important factors of this kind is the long time that it takes to construct industrial accommodation.

We shall now try to formulate more precisely the question of the effect that the construction period has on the development potential of industry. Let us denote by w the estimated cost, at constant prices, of all the projects under construction in a particular industry, at a particular time. Let θ stand for the length of the construction period, and i for the investment outlay per unit of time. Thus we have:

$$i = \frac{w}{\theta} \qquad (8)$$

It is thus necessary to complete $1/\theta$ of the contracted investments in each unit of time in order to complete all of them in the period θ. Therefore, with investments under contract amounting to w, investment outlays must equal w/θ in each unit of time.

When the value of investment projects rises, this construction period stays the same. Therefore investment outlays i will rise in proportion, as long as w does not exceed a certain critical value, w_{cr}. However, if the value of investments goes beyond this threshold, control over the investment process is lost, and the construction period starts to be prolonged. After a small further increase in w, a situation is arrived at in which θ grows in proportion to w, and therefore investment per unit of time ceases to rise.

This is illustrated graphically in Fig. 3, where w is on the horizontal

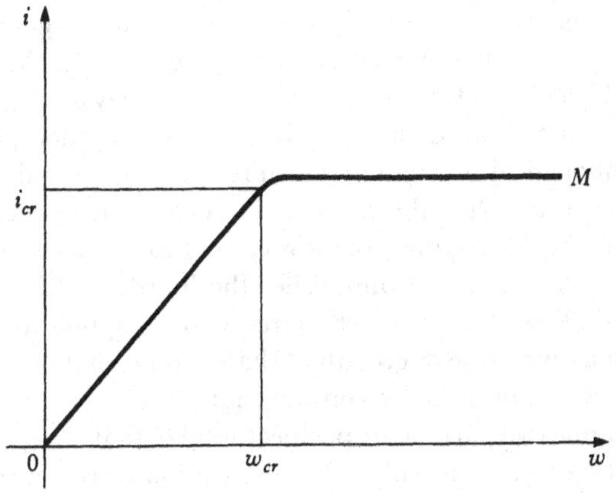

Figure 3

axis and i is on the vertical one. Where the curve OM is horizontal, any increase in w merely ties up more capital, and therefore has a detrimental effect. It turns out that it is not possible for investment to exceed a certain level of outlay i_{cr} that is defined by the equation:

$$i_{cr} = \frac{w_{cr}}{\theta} \tag{9}$$

The conclusion from this is that, given the technical and organisational possibilities of plant construction, realisable investments per unit of output are smaller the longer is the period of construction, θ. In this way, long construction periods have a damping effect on the development of a given industry.

However, it should be noted that, in reality, the rate of development of a given industry depends not on its investment outlay, but on the productive capacity created by that outlay. If we denote by m the coefficient of capital of investment, i.e., the amount of capital in that investment that is required to obtain a unit of productive capacity, then the equivalent investment, i, required for productive capacity z gives us:

$$z = \frac{i}{m} \tag{10}$$

Combining equations (9) and (10) we get

$$z_{cr} = \frac{i_{cr}}{m}, = \frac{w_{cr}}{\theta . m} \tag{11}$$

This formula shows that, with a given technical and organisational capacity for plant construction, i.e., with a given w_{cr}, the feasible investment effect on productive capacity, z, is inversely proportional to the coefficient of capital intensity, m, and the construction period, θ.

Thus, technological innovation which reduces the capital-intensity of investment, or abridges the construction cycle of new plant, *ceteris paribus* enables the development of the given industry to be accelerated. (Moreover, such innovation diminishes the 'burden' of investment, and therefore allows for a greater share of consumption in national income, with a given rate of growth of that income, or a faster rate of growth with the same share of consumption.)

Let us examine two parts of the perspective plan that are currently of great importance, and in which the application of the appropriate technology could contribute to reducing m, as well as shortening θ, thereby widening the bottlenecks affecting the development of particular industries. We have in mind here the construction of less massive factories, and changes in the methods of opening up new coal-mines.

II

It is well known that Polish expenditure on the building of industrial plants is disproportionately high in relation to the value of their productive equipment. In this respect, enormous progress has been made in the United States over recent decades. From 1929 to 1953, the share of buildings in productive fixed capital, at constant prices, has fallen from 65% to 53%.

Savings in construction may be obtained by leaving many industrial installations out in the open; by carefully planning the whole project and its construction, and especially designing spatial arrangements to make use of opportunities to reduce the costs of putting up buildings; by using the appropriate building materials; by avoiding every kind of 'monumentalism' and striving for unnecessary durability; and so on. It is clear that making the basic construction cheaper leads to reduced capital-intensity in investment, and this is achieved without reducing the productivity of labour.

The construction period in Poland is exceptionally long, and many times longer even than that in the United States. Efforts undertaken to make the basic construction less costly will, as a rule, automatically have the effect of shortening its construction period. Nevertheless, even better results may be obtained by designing the project in such a way as to enable it to be built as quickly as possible. Obviously, the abbreviation of the construction period depends to a great extent as well on improvements in and the mechanisation of the building work. But the introduction of these improvements requires an incomparably longer time than changes in project design which can be implemented immediately.

The use of less costly and more rapidly built industrial premises can contribute to a considerable reduction in m and θ. Similarly, it can alleviate development bottlenecks in many industries. The latter, as we have already stated, can have a considerable influence on speeding up the rate of economic growth.

Our second example of how industrial construction may be made more efficient is in deep coal-mining. The latest methods of opening up new pits aim to increase production per area of the coal-face. This means that there is a more rapid rate of extraction of the mine's reserves, and less time is spent in transporting them from the coal-face to the bottom of the lift-shaft. There are two ways of doing this:

(1) A shaft of normal capacity serves a considerably smaller coal-face area, as a result of which there is less need for underground transport.

(2) A shaft of considerably greater capacity serves a normal-sized coal-face area, but transport is speeded up with a more rapid movement of the cars.

Capital outlays per unit of production in both of these cases are less than those of existing mines, due to the lower costs of building underground roadways in relation to the amount extracted, while these roadways also allow for a more rapid rate of extraction. This is obtained at no cost in terms of labour productivity. On the contrary, productivity increases considerably, due mainly to the reduction in the number of workers employed in transporting coal in relation to those employed at the actual coal-face, but also due to easier access to the workface. (This last is the result of a reduction in the length of underground roadways in the case of the first kind of innovation. In the second case, it is because of the possibility of using air-shafts at the periphery of the area mined in order to enter and leave the pit.)

The period of construction in both cases is shorter. In the first system this is also because shorter underground roadways are used. It turns out that here it is also possible to mine higher seams, while simultaneously carrying out the work necessary to open up the next seam down. With the second system, it is mainly the ventilation shafts at the periphery of the area mined that, by allowing the underground roadways to be bored from both ends, contribute to shortening the construction cycle.

All this leads to very significant reductions in the product $m.\theta$. As a result, the introduction of these new systems of mining coal would enable the rate of growth of bituminous coal extraction in the perspective plan to be greatly increased. The resulting export potential would have a considerable effect on the balance of trade in the future. A faster increase in imports of raw materials and semi-fabricates would be possible in the perspective plan, which in turn would enable the rate of growth of national income to be raised.

10 The Influence of the Construction Period on the Relationship between Investment and National Income*

I

In 'The Growth of Investment and National Income in a Socialist Economy'† we abstracted away from the length of time that it takes to build investment projects. This was done for the sake of simplicity and, as a result, we also abstracted away from the difference between investment outlays in a given year and the volume of investments entering into production in that year.

In this article, we introduce this difference as a factor in the formula linking the increase in national income with investment. We shall show that this difference does not change the results obtained in our previous analysis, as long as the construction period remains constant.‡ At the same time, the modified equation for the growth rate of national income and investment throws light on the question of the coefficient of tied-up capital. The introduction of this coefficient enables us to allow for the tying up of capital during the construction period in our analysis of investment efficiency.

II

The basic equation that was introduced in the paper on the growth of investment and national income was presented as follows:

$$\Delta Y = \frac{1}{m} . I - a . Y + u . Y \qquad (1)$$

* First published in *Ekonomista*, 1957, No. 1, 3–13.

† See above pp. 70–83.

‡ This is an approximate formulation. As we shall see below, this condition is in fact somewhat more complicated.

where Y stands for the level of national income in a given year at constant prices; ΔY is the increase in national income that takes place between the beginning and the end of that year; I is investment in that year, also in constant prices; m stands for the investment outlay necessary in the given technical conditions to obtain a unit increase in national income; a is the coefficient of depreciation of productive capacity, showing the effect of obsolescence and of the wear and tear of productive equipment; finally, u is the coefficient of growth of national income that is due to improvements in labour organisation, greater economies in the use of raw materials and so on.

In equation (1) we have the three components of national income growth, ΔY. These are (1) the productive effect of current investment, namely $(1/m) . I$; (2) the negative effect of the contraction in productive capacity due to ageing, wear and tear, i.e., $-a . Y$; and (3) the effect of improvements that are independent of investment outlays, i.e., $u . Y$.

Dividing both sides of equation (1) by Y we get:

$$\frac{\Delta Y}{Y}=\frac{1}{m}.\frac{I}{Y}-a+u \tag{2}$$

It follows from equation (2) that, in fact, I represents here not the investment outlays in a given year, but the value of the investment projects entering production in that year, since only at this stage do investments have a productive effect. In our previous paper, where we abstracted away from the question of the construction period, investment outlays were identified with I. Consumption, in its broad sense,* C, was obtained by deducting I and the increase in working capital, S, from national income, Y.

In order to determine the relationship between the increase in national income and investment outlays in a given year, it is necessary to take into account the differences, arising because of the construction period, between those outlays and the projects entering production. Let J represent the outlay on investments in a given year, while I now stands for the volume of new projects entering into production in that year. The difference between these two magnitudes depends on changes in the amount of capital tied up in construction. If we denote the latter by B, we have:

$$J-I=\Delta B \tag{3}$$

* I.e., consumer investment, and defence production, as well as consumption in the strict sense of the word.

Since the capital under construction in each year is increased by the investment outlay, J, but is decreased by the number of completed projects handed over for productive use, the difference between these two magnitudes is the increase in capital under construction.

Thus we get:

$$I = J - \Delta B$$

Substituting this into equation (2), we get:

$$\frac{\Delta Y}{Y} = \frac{1}{m} \cdot \frac{J - \Delta B}{Y} - a + u \tag{4}$$

In this equation, instead of completed investment projects, I, we now have investment outlays, J. However, there now appears another factor, which is the increase in capital under construction, ΔB. Because of this, in order to be able to use this formula in analysing national income and investment growth, it is necessary to deal with the connection between the amount of capital under construction, and investment outlays, J.

III

Let us now introduce one more concept, that of the volume of investment orders. This is the planned cost of all investment projects under way at a given moment, which have been started but not completed. It is precisely because these projects are not completed, that the value of the capital tied up in them, B, is obviously smaller than Z. Let us suppose for the time being and for the sake of simplicity, that the construction time, ϕ, is the same for all projects, and that construction proceeds at a uniform rate, so that $1/\phi$ of each project's value is completed in each unit of time.

There is a simple relationship now between the volume of investment orders, Z, and investment outlays, J. This is:

$$J = \frac{Z}{\phi}$$

Since, during each unit of time, $1/\phi$ of the value of every other contracted investment is completed, with a volume of orders equal to Z, the investment outlay must equal Z/ϕ. The result is that:

$$Z = \phi . J \tag{5}$$

Therefore, if we determine the relationship between the capital under construction, B, and the volume of investment orders, Z, we can thereby explain the relationship between B and the investment outlay J.

As we have already stated, B is smaller than Z because not all the contracted projects that make up Z are completed. A project which has been under construction for nearly ϕ units of time is almost finished, and thefore the capital which is embodied in it is almost equal to the full value of the investment. By contrast, the capital tied up in a project that has only just been started will be almost equal to zero.

Let us suppose that we are using small units of time, such as months or quarters. We can then assume that the ϕ in each of these time units is expressed in absolute numbers. We shall investigate the coefficient of the capital contained in the projects started in ϕ successive units of time, up to a given moment, These will be fractions whose numerator is time, counted from the mid-point of the time unit, up to the given moment, and whose denominator is the whole construction period ϕ:

$$\frac{\phi-\frac{1}{2}}{\phi}, \frac{\phi-\frac{3}{2}}{\phi}, \frac{\phi-\frac{5}{2}}{\phi}, \ldots, \frac{\frac{1}{2}}{\phi}$$

It is easy to see that the average of these coefficients is equal to one-half. This is due to the fact that B is equal to half of Z if the total value of the projects started in each period is the same, i.e., if investment activity continues at a constant level. For *this* case in particular we therefore have:

$$\frac{B}{Z}=\frac{1}{2} \tag{6}$$

If investment per unit of time is continually rising, then this ratio no longer holds. If, however, the rate of growth is not too great, then it gives a reasonably good first approximation. If, for instance, investment is rising at an annual rate of 10%, then the ratio of B to Z is easily calculated as 0.49.

Combining equations (5) and (6) we get:

$$B=\tfrac{1}{2}.\phi.J \tag{7}$$

This equation can be represented differently if we introduce the concept of the period of tied up capital, τ.

Let us examine the construction of one project. In each of ϕ units of time, $1/\phi$ of the project's value will be completed. The part that is completed in the first time unit will be 'frozen' for a period of time, $\phi-\frac{1}{2}$, that part that is completed in the second period will be frozen for $\phi-(3/2)$ time units, and so on. The respective periods during which the particular sections of the project will be frozen will therefore be as follows:

$$\phi-\frac{1}{2}, \phi-\frac{3}{2}, \phi-\frac{5}{2}, \ldots, \frac{1}{2}$$

The period during which capital is tied up in the whole project can be defined as the mean period during which capital is tied up in its individual parts, weighted by their respective share of the value of the project. This is:

$$\tau=\frac{1}{\phi}\left(\phi-\frac{1}{2}\right)+\frac{1}{\phi}\left(\phi-\frac{3}{2}\right)+\frac{1}{\phi}\left(\phi-\frac{5}{2}\right)+\ldots+\frac{1}{\phi}\cdot\frac{1}{2}$$

As we have seen, the mean of these fractions is equal to $\frac{1}{2}$, and their sum equals $\phi\,.\,(\frac{1}{2})$. We thus have:

$$\tau=\frac{1}{2}\cdot\phi \tag{8}$$

Substituting this into equation (7), we get:

$$B=\tau\,.\,J \tag{9}$$

IV

Let us now remove our assumption that the construction of all projects proceeds uniformly, i.e., that during each unit of time $1/\phi$ of the value of the project is completed. In the ϕ succesive units of time, the parts of the project that are completed are given by the following array of fractions:

$$p_1, p_2, \ldots, p_\phi$$

The sum of this array is obviously equal to unity. Let us assume that this array will be the same for all investment projects. The fraction of total capital started in successive periods of time will now be:

$$p_1\left(\phi-\frac{1}{2}\right), p_2\left(\phi-\frac{3}{2}\right), p_3\left(\phi-\frac{5}{2}\right), \ldots, p_\phi\cdot\frac{1}{2}$$

The arithmetic mean of this sequence will be:

$$\frac{p_1(\phi-\frac{1}{2}), p_2(\phi-\frac{3}{2}), p_3(\phi-\frac{5}{2})+\ldots+p_\phi\cdot\frac{1}{2}}{\phi}$$

This mean will be smaller than unity, depending on the contents of the array:

$$p_1, p_2, p_3, \ldots, p_\phi$$

i.e., depending on how construction of the project proceeds over time. Let us denote this mean by k. If the value of the projects started in each unit of time is the same, i.e., if investment activity is maintained at a constant level, then the ratio of capital tied up in construction, B, to the total value of contracted investments, Z, is equal to k:

$$\frac{B}{Z}=k \tag{10}$$

In the case of $p_1=p_2=\ldots=p_\phi=1/\phi$, which we examined above, $k=\frac{1}{2}$.

As for the relationship between the value of investment orders and general investment outlays, J, the equation

$$Z=\phi . J \tag{5}$$

still holds, if investment activity remains at a constant level. In fact, in each of the successive units of time leading up to a certain moment, the construction of projects of exactly the same value, namely Z/ϕ, is commenced. The projects started in the first unit of time are now in their final stage of construction, so that the work done on them per unit of time is $p\phi$ (Z/ϕ). The projects started in the second unit of time are now in their penultimate stage of construction, so that the outlay on them per unit of time is $p_{\phi-1}$ (Z/ϕ) and so on. We therefore have the following sequence of outlays on the projects started in each of the units of time:

$$p_\phi\cdot\frac{Z}{\phi}, p_{\phi-1}\cdot\frac{Z}{\phi}, \ldots, p_1\cdot\frac{Z}{\phi}$$

The sum of these outlays is equal to the general investment outlay per unit of time, J. Since

$$p_1+p_2+\ldots+p_\phi=1$$

we get

$$J=\frac{Z}{\phi}, \text{ or, } Z=\phi . J \tag{5}$$

Combining this with equation (10) we arrive at:

$$B=k.\phi.J \tag{11}$$

This is the generalised version of equation (7).

This relationship was arrived at under the assumption of a constant level of investment activity. Even if investment rises at a moderate rate, equation (11) will still provide a good first approximation.

In this case too we can express this formula in a different form, by introducing the length of time during which capital is tied up, τ. Again, let us examine the construction of one project. As in the particular case considered previously, the respective periods during which the individual parts of the project are tied up are:

$$\phi-\frac{1}{2}, \phi-\frac{3}{2}, \phi-\frac{5}{2}, \ldots, \frac{1}{2}$$

But the respective parts of the project are now no longer equal in value, but are expressed as the sequence of fractions:

$$p_1, p_2, p_3, \ldots, p_\phi$$

Therefore, the period during which the capital of the project is tied up comes to:

$$\tau=p_1\left(\phi-\frac{1}{2}\right)+p_2\left(\phi-\frac{3}{2}\right)+p_3\left(\phi-\frac{5}{2}\right)+\ldots+p_\phi\frac{1}{2}$$

The result obtained is none other than the numerator of the fraction defining k. We therefore have:

$$\tau=k.\phi$$

Combining this with equation (11) we get:

$$B=\tau.J$$

We thus get the same equation as was arrived at in our previous examination of investment in a particular project.

So far we have assumed that the construction period and the progress of work during it, and therefore also the mean period during which capital is tied up, τ, are the same for all projects. In reality, as we know, this is not so. But if the weighting of the values of projects that are tied up for the same length of time in investments under contract does not vary significantly, the equation (9) remains a valid approximation.

V

Let us now return to equation (4):

$$\frac{\Delta Y}{Y}=\frac{1}{m}\cdot\frac{J-\Delta B}{Y}-a+u$$

For the increase in capital under construction, ΔB tied up for a constant mean period, τ, we get from equation (9) the value:*

$$\Delta B=\tau.\Delta J$$

Substituting this for the value of ΔB in equation (4) we get:

$$\frac{\Delta Y}{Y}=\frac{1}{m}\cdot\frac{J-\tau.\Delta J}{Y}-a+u \qquad (12)$$

Taking J outside brackets and multiplying $\tau.\Delta J$ by J/Y, we get:

$$\frac{\Delta Y}{Y}=\frac{1}{m}\cdot\frac{J}{Y}\left(1-\tau\frac{\Delta J}{Y}\right)-a+u \qquad (12)$$

This equation shows the way in which the rate of growth of national income depends on the share of investment in that income, and on the rate of growth of investment.

Let us recall that national income, Y, includes investment outlays, J, increases in working capital,† which we denote by S, and consumption in the broad sense, C, which includes consumer investments, production for defence purposes, and finally, consumption in the strict sense.

* It should be reiterated here that equation (9) is only an approximation. As we have seen, strictly speeaking it should be:

$$B=b.\tau.J$$

where b approaches unity, if the rate of growth is not too fast. If the rate of growth of investment is constant, then b is also constant. In this case, ΔB is exactly equal to $b.\tau.\Delta J$, and therefore may be said to be equal to $\tau.\Delta J$, as a reasonable approximation. However, if the rate of growth of investment is not constant, then the coefficient a also varies, and therefore the formula $\Delta B=\tau.\Delta J$ will only provide a good approximation when changes in the rate of growth are gradual.

† Because the ΔB contained in J includes the whole of the increase in the capital involved in construction, changes in production under way in the machine industry should be excluded from the increase in working capital, S.

(We assume that imports and exports are balanced.) We therefore have:

$$Y=J+S+C \tag{13}$$

Next, let us assume that increases in working capital are directly proportionate to the increase in national income, so that they equal:

$$S=n.\Delta Y \tag{14}$$

Hence we get the share of consumption in national income, which is:

$$\frac{C}{Y}=1-\frac{J}{Y}-n.\frac{\Delta Y}{Y} \tag{15}$$

VI

It follows from equation (12) that if investment outlays and national income rise at the same rate, then this rate is constant. In fact, in this case we have, first of all:

$$\frac{\Delta Y}{Y}=\frac{\Delta J}{J}$$

And therefore equation (12) becomes:

$$\frac{\Delta Y}{Y}=\frac{1}{m}.\left(1-r\frac{\Delta Y}{Y}\right)\frac{J}{Y}-a+u$$

Furthermore, since J and Y rise at the same rate, J/Y, the share of investment in national income is constant. It follows from this that the relative increase in national income is also constant. We can therefore state that increasing investment outlays and national income at the same rate secures uniform expanded reproduction.

From equation (15) it follows that consumption, C, rises at the same rate as national income. Since J/Y and $\Delta Y/Y$ are constant, then C/Y also remains unchanged.

Let us now suppose that investment outlays J rise faster than national income. From equation (12) it follows that in this case $\Delta J/J$ would stay constant, but J/Y would rise. But according to equation (12) this means a rise in $\Delta Y/Y$, i.e., a relative increase in national income. A growth of investment outlays that is faster than that of national income thus leads to an acceleration in the growth of that income.

In the above discussion, we assumed that coefficients m, a, n, u, and the mean construction time ϕ stay constant. However, if there is technical progress of a predominantly capital-intensive kind, then m will rise continually. In this case then, a uniform growth of investment outlays and national income at the same rate cannot be maintained. In fact, in equation (12), J/Y and $\Delta J/J$ would still remain constant. But with a rising m, this would mean a fall in $\Delta Y/Y$, i.e., a drop in the rate of growth of national income. If a steady rate of economic growth is aimed at, then it is necessary for investment outlays to rise faster than national income.

The share of consumption in national income, C/Y, would fall in both the cases examined above. When the growth of investment outlays is faster than that of national income, with a constant m, this leads to an acceleration in economic growth, in which J/Y as well as $\Delta Y/Y$ will rise and, thus, according to equation (15), C/Y will diminish. In the case of steady growth of national income, with a rising m, investment outlays again rise faster than national income. J/Y will rise, but $\Delta Y/Y$ will stay constant. Hence, here too C/Y will fall.

The analysis that we have conducted shows that allowing for a period of time for the construction of investment projects does not invalidate the conclusions regarding the growth of investment and national income that we reached in our previous analysis. As was stated at the beginning, we shall now attempt to use equation (12) to resolve the question of the coefficient of tied-up capital.

VII

Let us re-write equation (12),

$$\frac{\Delta Y}{Y}=\frac{1}{m}\left(1-\tau\frac{\Delta J}{J}\right)\frac{J}{Y}-a+u$$

in the abbreviated form:

$$\frac{\Delta Y}{Y}=\frac{1}{m'}\cdot\frac{J}{Y}-a+u$$

$$\text{where } m'=\frac{m}{1-\tau.\dfrac{\Delta J}{J}}$$

Let us suppose that the mean period during which capital is tied up in construction, τ, has been prolonged, without any increase in the rate of growth of investment, $\Delta J/J$. It is clear that the resulting increase in the fraction:

$$\frac{1}{1-\tau.\frac{\Delta J}{J}}$$

affects m' in the same way as an increase in investment outlays per unit of output, m. In other words, the rise in $1/(1-\tau.(\Delta J/J))$, that is the result of lengthening the average period during which capital is tied up in construction, affects the relationship between the growth of investment and national income in the same way as an increase in the capital-intensity of investment. The greater is m or $1/(1-\tau.(\Delta J/J))$, the greater must be the share of investment, J/Y, necessary to obtain a given rate of growth of national income, $\Delta Y/Y$.

It is apparent that these results may be applied in analysing the efficiency of investment. Let us accept the growth rate of investment, $\Delta J/J$, as given, and denote it by r. We thus have:

$$m' = \frac{m}{1-\tau.r}$$

Let us suppose that we are examining a certain investment project requiring a capital of m_1 per unit of productive capacity in the new plant. The period during which this project will be tied up in construction will be τ_1.

We can calculate m'_1 for this project on the basis of the following equation:

$$m'_1 = \frac{m_1}{1-\tau_1.r}$$

It is clear that a lower m'_1 corresponding to a lower share of this project in investment overall will tend to reduce m' for the economy as a whole. In turn, the reduced outlay per unit of production, m, in this project, and the reduction in the fraction $1/(1-\tau_1.r)$, thanks to the reduced period during which capital is tied up, will have a similar effect on the relationship between the growth of investment and national income. For this reason, in analysing the efficiency of investment for various projects, their $m'_1 = m_1/(1-\tau_1.r)$ should be compared, rather than their m_1. In other words, in order to allow for the period during which capital is tied up in construction, the necessary capital should be divided by $(1-\tau_1.r)$.

Therefore we have as the coefficient of capital tied up in construction:

$$\lambda = \frac{1}{1 - \tau_1 . r}$$

This is the fraction by which the value of an investment project should be increased in order to allow for the tying up of capital in construction.

The following example illustrates the coefficient of capital tied up in construction. A project valued at 4 million złoty is to be built over a period of three years. The specifications anticipate outlays of zł1 million, in the first and second years, and zł2 millons in the third year. The average period during which this capital is tied up amounts to:

$$\tau_1 = \frac{(1 \times 2.5) + (1 \times 1.5) + (2 \times 0.5)}{4} = 1.25$$

Let us suppose that the rate of growth of investment in our present circumstances comes to 10% per annum, i.e., $r = 0.10$.

Therefore, the coefficient of tied up capital is calculated as:

$$\lambda = \frac{1.25 \times 0.10}{1 - (1.25 \times 0.10)} = 0.14$$

This means that, in order to account for the capital that will be tied up in construction, 14% should be added to the value of the project, i.e., it should be increased from zł4 millions to zł4.56 millions.

11 On the Coefficient of Capital Tied Up in Construction*

I

By the coefficient of tied-up capital, we mean here the percentage by which the value of an investment project should be increased, in analysing the efficiency of that investment, in order to allow for the period of time during which capital outlays are tied up in construction. I have already discussed this question in my article 'The Influence of the Construction Period on the Relationship between Investment and National Income', in connection with an investigation of the effect that the construction period has on the growth relationship between investment and national income.

The formulation of the issue which I presented there, broadly speaking, is as follows. When investment, I, rises, the capital tied up in construction rises more or less proportionately, given a certain construction period. Therefore, part of the investment is then allocated not to expanding the productive apparatus, but to increasing the amount of capital that is tied up. If the construction period is very short, then the volume of equipment entering production in a given year would be virtually equal to the investment outlay in that year. The same would apply if investment was maintained at a constant level. But when the construction period is not very short, and when investment outlays, J, are continually rising, part of J is always absorbed by the increase in tied-up capital. Therefore, investment outlays are correspondingly less efficient, and on this basis it is possible to introduce a formula for the coefficient of tied up capital.

* First published in *Ekonomista*, no. 6, 1958 1393–1400.

Already as I was writing that article, I was aware that such an approach does not deal with the whole issue. If the construction period is shortened, this not only makes future investment more efficient, in the sense defined above, but also has an immediate effect in reducing capital already tied up in construction. In particular, when investment is maintained at a constant level, the coefficient of tied-up capital calculated by my previous method equals zero, because it depends on *increases* in tied-up capital, and thus on the growth of J. But it is in just such a case that a gain is obtained through the reduction in the construction time, inasmuch as some amount of capital is released. But this gain is only obtained once. If we use it to reduce investment and increase consumption correspondingly during a certain period, then, after this period of abatement, there will be a return to the previous state of affairs: A one-off saving in productive capital will not leave any lasting trace on the process of economic development. It is precisely this that justifies leaving out this effect in the calculation of the coefficient of tied-up capital.

However, when I returned to this question, I noticed that there is another possible solution. A one-off saving of productive capital may be used not for a temporary reduction in investment for the benefit of consumption, but to increase *permanently* national income. It is this that is the starting point for this article. In it I shall try to formulate in a more definitive way than before the problem of the effect of tied-up capital on the efficiency of investment.

II

Let us examine a certain process of economic development. Let I_t and Y_t stand for gross productive investment and gross national income in time t. The capital that is tied up at time t will equal approximately τI_t, where τ is the period during which capital is tied up, i.e., the average length of time during which successively completed parts of the investment project are tied up.* When the construction of the project proceeds at a uniform rate, τ is equal to half of the construction period. Obviously, the construction period of investment projects is not the same for all projects. Therefore, when we state that for the economy as a whole the capital tied up in construction is equal to τI_t, by τ we mean

* See 'The Influence of the Construction Period on the Relationship between Investment and National Income' above, pp. 97–108.

the weighted mean of all the periods during which capital is tied up in the respective projects.

Let us suppose that the construction period is so shortened that capital is virtually not tied up at all. Therefore, if investment outlays are maintained at a constant level of I_t, then the productive apparatus will increase at the moment t by the amount τI_t. This increase in productive equipment allows national income to be increased. Obviously it would be necessary to employ additional manpower to operate the additional equipment. But for the time being, let us assume that some labour reserve exists, in which case the issue of employment does not present any difficulties. (Later on we shall examine a situation in which additional mechanisation is necessary to resolve this problem.)

We shall denote by m the capital-intensity of the increase in national income resulting from the new productive capacity.* It follows from what has been stated above that at a given time t national income rises by $(1/m)\tau I_t$, as a consequence of the 'release' of this capital.

It should be noted that the increase in productive capacity arising from the release of capital also has a certain effect on investment. In fact, this additional capacity will gradually wear out. To overcome this, it will be necessary to make provisions in total investment for additional depreciation. If we denote the coefficient of depreciation by a, then the additional depreciation will amount to $a.\tau.I_t$. (*Maintaining* investment, I_t, at a constant level is necessary to make use of the capital released by increasing productive capacity. But the *wearing out* of this additional capacity requires an increase in investment of $a.\tau.I_t$.)

However, this is not the end of the matter. Productive apparatus not only wears out, but its productivity also rises as a result of improvements in its use (through better work organisation, economies in raw materials usage, and so on). This is the opposite process to that of the wearing out of fixed capital.† Thus, if we denote the coefficient of these improvements by u, then investment may be *reduced* as a result of improvements in the use of the additional productive capacity by $u.\tau.I_t$.

The results of this discussion can be summed up as follows.

Let us call the actual process of investment and production the *primary* process; and the actual growth process obtained from the release of capital under construction the *secondary* process. We shall denote productive investment and national income in that *secondary*

* *Ibid* p. 98. † *Ibid.*

process by I'_t and Y'_t. We therefore have the following relationship between these variables, and the variables I_t and Y_t in the *primary* process:

$$I'_t = I_t + \tau . a . I_t - \tau . u . I_t \tag{1}$$

$$Y'_t = Y_t + \frac{\tau . I_t}{m} \tag{2}$$

Subtracting equation (2) from equation (1), we get

$$Y'_t - I'_t = (Y_t - I_t) + \tau . I_t \left(\frac{1}{m} - a + u\right) \tag{3}$$

We can see that the difference between national income and productive investment in the *secondary* process is greater than that in the *primary* process by:

$$\tau . I_t \left(\frac{1}{m} - a + u\right)$$

III

Let us now imagine that, in the *secondary* process, an increase in capital intensity occurs, from m to m'', but that the growth of national income stays the same. For this condition to be satisfied, investment will have to rise according to the ratio m''/m, as a result of which $Y - I$ will obviously be reduced. Let us further assume that m'' is now set at that level at which $Y - I$ is reduced to the same level as that in the *primary* process. In this way, we get a *tertiary* process. Let us denote investment and national income at time t in the *tertiary* process by I''_t and Y''_t. We then get:

$$I''_t = \frac{m''}{m} . I'_t \tag{4}$$

and

$$Y''_t = Y'_t \tag{5}$$

Hence we get:

$$Y''_t - I''_t = Y'_t - \frac{m''}{m} I'_t$$

or

$$Y''_t - I''_t = Y'_t - I'_t - \left(\frac{m''}{m} - 1\right) I'_t \tag{6}$$

Thus, the reduction in the difference between the national income obtained in the *tertiary* process, and the productive investment in it, $Y-I$, compared to that in the *secondary* process, amounts to:

$$\left(\frac{m''}{m}-1\right)I'_t$$

Since, according to our assumption, this reduction in $Y-I$ is equal to the increase in $Y-I$ in the *secondary* process compared to the *primary* process, we get:

$$\tau . I_t\left(\frac{1}{m}-a+u\right)=\left(\frac{m''}{m}-1\right)I'_t \qquad (7)$$

Substituting for I'_t from equation (1), and rearranging, we get:

$$\frac{m''}{m}=\frac{\tau\left(\frac{1}{m}-a+u\right)}{1+\tau . a-\tau . u} \qquad (8)$$

Let us now compare the *tertiary* process with the *primary* one. The excess of national income over productive investment, $Y-I$, has the same value throughout in both processes. In the *tertiary* process, capital is not tied up in construction, but this is offset by a greater capital-intensity of investment. It is thus possible to state that the ratio of the capital-intensity in the two processes, m''/m, is a measure of the adverse effect of tied-up capital in the *primary* process: Both processes are equivalent in the sense that the difference between national income and investment, $Y-I$, is the same in both. However, in the *primary* process, capital is tied up in construction, while in the *tertiary* process there is greater capital-intensity. Therefore it can be assumed that the coefficient of tied-up capital, λ, for the economy as a whole is equal to $(m''-m)/m$. Thus, according to equation (8),

$$\lambda=\frac{\tau\left(\frac{1}{m}-a+u\right)}{1+\tau . a-\tau . u} \qquad (9)$$

Since, in general $\tau(a-u)$ will be very small, we can write as a good approximation:

$$\lambda=\tau\left(\frac{1}{m}-a+u\right) \qquad (10)$$

Doubt may be expressed as to whether the *primary* and the *tertiary* processes are fully equivalent, as it is this equivalence which lies at the basis of the above reasoning. This is because it is only the difference between national income and productive investment that is identical in both processes, but national income itself is greater in the *tertiary* process than it is in the *primary* process. However, it should be remembered that this greater output in the *tertiary* process consists solely of production by the same productive capacity at a greater cost.

IV

Equation (9) defines the coefficient of tied-up capital for the whole economy. What will this coefficient be for particular types of investment? Let us denote investments of a certain kind actually taking place (and therefore in the *primary* process) at time t by I_{It}, and the period during which they are tied up in construction by τ_I. Let us suppose now that the construction period in the industry producing investment goods is reduced to a very small amount. Let us assume that the capital thereby released is used in all industries to increase national income. Reasoning as we did previously, in examining investment overall, we find that productive capital has increased in time t by $\tau_I I_{It}$. Therefore, the difference between national income and investment will rise by

$$\tau_I I_{It}\left(\frac{1}{m} - a + u\right)$$

Let us now proceed to examine the increase in capital-intensity of the investment under consideration from m to m''. This increase in capital-intensity would absorb the above increase in the difference between national income and investment, while keeping national income on the same growth path as in the *secondary* process.

If we assume that in the *secondary* process investment overall is the same as in the *primary* process, then an investment of a particular type will change in the same proportion as the whole of investment in the *secondary* process, compared to overall investment in the *primary* process. From equation (1) it follows that investment overall changes by a factor equal to $1 + \tau . a - \tau . u$. Therefore, investment of the particular kind that we are examining in the *secondary* process will amount to $I_{It}(1 + \tau . a - \tau . u)$.

If we increase the capital-intensity of this investment from m to m'', then, to maintain national income on an unchanged growth path, investment must rise by a factor equal to m''_1/m_1, namely by:

$$I_{1t}(1+\tau.a-\tau.u)\left(\frac{m''_1}{m_1}-1\right)$$

For this increase in investment to absorb the increase in the difference between national income and investment, arising from the capital 'released' from construction in these particular projects, the following equation must hold:

$$\tau_1 I_{1t}\left(\frac{1}{m}-a+u\right)=I_{1t}(1+\tau.a-\tau.u)\left(\frac{m''_1}{m_1}-1\right) \qquad (11)$$

or

$$\frac{m''_1-m_1}{m_1}=\tau_1\frac{\frac{1}{m}-a+u}{1+\tau.a-\tau.u} \qquad (12)$$

Since the increase in capital-intensity absorbs the effect of the capital released by the reduction in construction time, $(m''_1-m_1)/m_1$ may be considered as the coefficient of tied-up capital, λ_1, for this kind of investment. Thus we get:

$$\lambda_1=\tau_1\frac{\frac{1}{m}-a+u}{1+\tau.a-\tau.u} \qquad (13)$$

and, after omitting the insignificant $\tau.(a-u)$ in the denominator:

$$\lambda_1=\tau_1\left(\frac{1}{m}-a+u\right) \qquad (14)$$

It should be stressed that coefficients *m*, *a* and *u* are characteristics of the economy as a whole, and not of a particular type of investment. This follows from our assumption that capital released in the particular kind of investment process is placed at the disposal of the economy as a whole, i.e., contributes to an increase in production in all sectors of the economy.

In the Polish perspective plan, the term in brackets comes to around 0.4, and *m* is equal to about 2.5, while $a-u$ is very small.* We would then get $\lambda_1=0.4\tau_1$.

However, it should be remembered here that, for the time being, we do not allow for any problems of labour shortages, which may arise in

* *m* was calculated on the basis of national income expressed in factory prices. It is this definition of national income, in which the effect on the prices of consumer goods of turnover tax is avoided, that is tacitly accepted in the above analysis.

raising national income through an increase in the productive equipment obtained by releasing capital under construction. Let us now turn to this issue.

V

Let us suppose that there are no labour reserves in the economy. Therefore, the additional productive equipment obtained from the 'release' of capital from construction cannot be manned through increasing mechanisation without releasing manpower in some part of the economy. In this way, part of the capital released will be absorbed by the investments necessary for mechanisation, and therefore the increase in national income will be less than we were able to obtain in our previous analysis.

Let us denote this increase by y. The outlays on mechanisation necessary to obtain the manpower needed to produce that increase, y, will be more or less proportional to y. They will amount to $j.y$, where j is a coefficient whose size depends on the increase in employment per unit increase in income, and on the mechanisation costs incurred in releasing one worker.

The whole of the capital released from construction, $\tau.I$, cannot now be used for the production of additional national output, but only $\tau.I.j.y$. This additional output will amount to $(\tau.I-j.y)/m$, so that we get

$$y=\frac{\tau.I-j.y}{m} \qquad (15)$$

Rearranging this we get:

$$y=\frac{\tau.I}{m+j}$$

If we proceed with our analysis now as we did previously, but substituting everywhere for the increase in national income, $(\tau.I)/m$, the term $(\tau.I)/(m+j)$, it can be seen that, at the end, we have the same formulae for the coefficient of tied-up capital, except that m is now replaced by $m+j$. Thus, for the economy as a whole, we get

$$\lambda=\tau_1.\frac{\frac{1}{m+j}-a+u}{1+\tau.a-\tau.u} \qquad (9')$$

and, as a good approximation,

$$\lambda = \tau . \left(\frac{1}{m+j} - a + u\right) \tag{10'}$$

For a given project we get

$$\lambda_1 = \tau_1 . \frac{\frac{1}{m+j} - a + u}{1 + \tau . a - \tau . u} \tag{13'}$$

and, as an approximate formula,

$$\lambda_1 = \tau_1 . \left(\frac{1}{m+j} - a + u\right) \tag{14'}$$

If there are adequate labour reserves, then $j = 0$, and in this special case, the previous formulae apply. However, it should be noted that this special case requires the availability of labour reserves throughout the whole of the growth process, and thus not just at present, but during the whole currency of a long-term plan.

For the Polish perspective plan, we can accept, as has already been stated, that approximately $m = 2.5$, and $a - u = 0$. However, it is difficult to estimate j. Let us assume that it will be somewhere between 1.5 and 2.5. Since pay constitutes a considerable part of the increase in national income at factory prices, this means that the pay-back period for mechanisation will be not much longer than 1.5 to 2.5 years.* For the lower boundary of j we get

$$\lambda_1 = 0.25 . \tau_1$$

and for the higher boundary of j, we get

$$\lambda_1 = 0.20 . \tau_1$$

These are coefficients for tied up capital that are significantly greater than those hitherto used in calculating investment efficiency.

* To produce a national income of y, a number of workers, l, are needed. Let us denote the worker's wage by w. As we have said, $w . l$ constitutes a considerable part of y. In order to release l workers, mechanisation is applied in some part of the economy. If we accept that workers' wages there are equal to w, and the pay-back period for outlays on mechanisation is denoted by n, then the outlays amount to $n . l . w$. Therefore, $j = (n . l . w)/y$. Since $l . w$ is somewhat smaller than y, n is somewhat greater than j.

Notes

1 Introduction

1 E.g., J. Goldmann & K. Kouba, *Economic Growth in Czechoslovakia*, White Plains USA, International Arts and Sciences Press 1969.

2 Socialist Clarity Group *Labour Discussion Notes*, no. 13 July 1940.

3 'The Essentials for Democratic Planning', the first essay in this volume.

4 J. Kaliński, *Plan odbudowy gospodarczej 1947–1949*, Warszawa, Książka i Wiedza 1977 pp. 116 and 202.

5 J.M. Montias, *Central Planning in Poland*, Yale University Press, New Haven 1962, chapter 3.

6 E.g., H. Minc, 'Przyczyny obecnych trudności w zaopatrzeniu i środki walki z tymi trudnościami', *Nowe Drogi* 1952, no. 28 lipiec-sierpień, pp. 12–24. Paranoia is not the exclusive property of Marxists or Stalinists. Mr Samuel Brittan recently blamed the difficulties of the Conservative government in Britain on the lack of total enthusiasm and understanding for the true meaning of monetarism among *named* senior civil servants and Government economists (*Financial Times*, 10 January 1985). Similar reasons are currently being advanced to explain the 'failure' of the 1981–3 economic reforms in Poland.

7 'Nie przeceniać roli modelu', *Trybuna Ludu*, 3 February 1957 no. 33, reproduced in Kalecki's Collected Works, *Dzieła*, vol. 3, Warszawa, Państwowe Wydawnictwo Ekonomiczne 1982 pp. 105–9.

8 A similar account of the role of over-centralisation under the first Soviet Five Year Plans has been given by E. Zaleski in *Planning for Economic Growth in the Soviet Union 1918–1932*, University of North Carolina Press, Chapel Hill 1971, p. 296.

9 See M. Kalecki, 'Outline of a Method of Constructing a Perspective Plan', in A. Nove and D.M. Nuti (eds.) *Socialist Economics*, Penguin, Harmondsworth 1972, pp. 213–22.

10 M. Rakowski, 'O tempie wzrostu gospodarki w planie perspektywicznym', *Gospodarka Planowa*, 1958 no. 10 pp. 29–35. See also J.M. Montias, *op. cit.*, pp. 157–9.

11 J.M. Montias, *ibid.*; M. Kalecki, 'The 1961–1975 Long-Run Economic Plan', *Polish Perspectives*, 1959 no. 3 pp. 3–19. For the most recent and thorough analysis of this plan, see J. Osiatyński, 'Michał Kalecki's Perspective Development Plan for Poland (1961–1975)', *Oeconomica Polonica*, 1982 no. 3–4 pp. 227–49.

12 M. Kalecki 'Workers' Councils and Central Planning' in this volume.

13 J. Kornai, *Economics of Shortage*, North-Holland Publishing Company, Amsterdam 1980, vol. A pp. 191–4. See also T. Bauer 'Investment Cycles in Planned Economies', *Acta Oeconomica* 1978 vol. 21 pp. 243–60.

[14] United Nations *Economic Survey of Europe in 1959*, Geneva 1960, chapter 2, pp. 2–3. The unfortunate effects of the good weather confirm the wisdom of the Polish peasant saying that the country suffers from four recurrent natural disasters: spring, summer, autumn and winter.

[15] United Nations, *Economic Survey of Europe in 1960*, Geneva 1961, pp. 92–3.

[16] An account of this is given in J. Toporowski, 'Crisis and Reform in the Polish Economy: A Note on the Relevance of Planning and Workers' Control in the Current Crisis', paper presented at a Socialist Environment and Resources Association Conference on Trades Unions, Self-Management and Socialism: The Polish Experience, held at Ruskin College, Oxford, 17 October 1981 (unpublished).

[17] J. Kornai, *ibid.*

[18] E.g., F.A. von Hayek, 'The Uses of Knowledge in Society', *American Economic Review* 1945, vol. 35, no. 4 pp. 519–30.

[19] See A. Zauberman, *Industrial Progress in Poland, Czechoslovakia and East Germany 1937–1962*, Oxford University Press 1964, and A. Karpiński, *Gospodarcza pozycja Polski w świecie*, Warszawa Książka i Wiedza, 1973

[20] See especially the essay on 'Problems in the Theory of Growth of a Socialist Economy', in this volume. This view is enlarged upon in W. Brus & K. Łaski, 'Growth at the Full Employment of Productive Forces', in *Problems of Economic Dynamics and Planning: Essays in Honour of Michał Kalecki*, Warszawa Państwowe Wydawnictwo Naukowe 1964. Janos Kornai presents this view in *Anti-Equilibrium: On Economic Systems Theory and the Tasks of Research*, North–Holland Publishing Company, Amsterdam 1971.

[21] Cf. Hyman P. Minsky, 'The Financial Instability Hypothesis: A Restatement', *Thames Papers in Political Economy*, Thames Polytechnic, London 1978.

[22] Cf. E.V.K. Fitzgerald, 'The Problem of Balance in the Peripheral Socialist Economy: A Conceptual Note', *World Development* 1985, vol. 13 pp. 5–14.

[23] This distinction is developed in J. Toporowski, 'Sources of Disequilibrium in a Centrally Planned Economy', unpublished PhD thesis, Birmingham University 1983, chapter 9.

[24] Cf. M. Kalecki, *Selected Essays on the Economic Growth of the Socialist and the Mixed Economy*, Cambridge University Press 1979, chapter 9.

[25] See M. Rakowski, *op. cit.*

[26] M. Kalecki, *Selected Essays*, chapter 1. A detailed presentation of the Material Product System of national accounts is given in L. Zieńkowski, *Podstawowe założenia bilansu gospodarki narodowej*, Warszawa, Glówny Urząd Statystyczny, 1968.

[27] M. Kalecki, *Essays on Developing Economies*, The Harvester Press, Hassocks, Sussex 1976.

[28] See especially 'Central Price Determination as an Essential Feature of a Socialist Economy', in this volume.

[29] See note 24.

3 Workers' Councils and Central Planning

[1] Law on Workers' Councils dated 19 November 1956, *Dziennik Ustaw* 1956, no. 53, art. 238; See also J.G. Zieliński, *Economic Reforms in Polish Industry*, London, Oxford University Press 1973 pp. 235–8.

[2] The condition for overall balance in the consumer goods markets is that the wage bill in department I (where means of production are produced) is equal to the surplus obtained from department II (where means of consumption are produced). Clearly therefore incomes in both sectors need careful coordination. See K. Łaski, 'Warunki równowagi ogólnej między produkcją a spożyciem w gospodarce socjalistycznej', in O. Lange (ed.), *Zagadnienia ekonomii politycznej socjalizmu*, Warszawa, Książka i Wiedza 1960 pp. 176–237.

[3] These drawbacks centre around the way in which gross output targets encourage excessive production in every sense of the term, wasting materials, producing unmarketable output, and discouraging the efficient use of resources. From the late 1950s onwards, increasing weight has been attached to the other, more refined targets. But perhaps because of the way in which they fit in conveniently with the enduring system of planning by commodity balances, gross output targets have never been altogether abandoned in Eastern Europe. See also A. Zauberman, *Industrial Progress in Poland Czechoslovakia and East Germany*, London, Oxford University Press 1964, pp. 110–14. In 1964 in Polish industry 'gross value indices were still used in 82% of all industrial enterprises, producing 77% of total industrial output. Physical and net output indices were used in the remaining 18%' (J.G. Zieliński, *op. cit.*, p. 123).

[4] In the 1960s, various net output targets were introduced for Polish state enterprises, although generally alongside, rather than instead of, gross output targets. See references in note 3 above.

[5] 'Synthetic' indicators are value indicators of economic activity. Their main advantage lies in the fact that they can be used to measure and add up physically incommensurable production processes. The most common 'synthetic' indicator is the profit obtained from different activities. As Kalecki points out, their main disadvantage is that they may not distinguish adequately between the circumstances or functions of different activities.

[6] From the 1950s onwards, a shortage of labour has been the main factor inhibiting the development of Polish coal-mining. This in turn was not due to an overall shortage of labour throughout the economy, but to inadequate housing and social infrastructure in the main coal-mining region of Silesia. In agriculture, the labour problem on Polish state farms is also a sectoral one. It arises from the situation of state farms mainly in the formerly German areas in the North and West of present-day Poland. These areas were settled with a Polish population largely after the War, but the urban economy generally, and the construction industry in particular, proved more attractive to mobile labour. See C. Bobrowski, 'Stopień swobody wyboru: Uwagi na marginesie wytycznych rozwoju gospodarczego na lata 1961–1965', *Gospodarka Planowa* 1959, no. 1–2, pp. 5–9, and A. Karpinski, *Polityka uprzemysłowienia Polski w latach 1958–1968*, Warszawa, Państwowe Wydawnictwo Ekonomiczne 1969, pp. 166–8.

[7] In a subsequent (1964) edition of this essay that appeared in his collection of essays, *Z zagadnień gospodarczo-społecznych Polski Ludowej*, Warszawa, Państwowe Wydawnictwo Naukowe 1964, Kalecki omitted the previous six paragraphs.

[8] Polish agriculture is largely in private hands and technically backward by European standards. Thus, the availability of greater supplies of building materials in rural areas would encourage greater agricultural production, whose sale would realise the wherewithal to purchase more building materials.

[9] See note 6.

[10] This summary of the Law on Workers' Councils was originally included by Kalecki in the French translation of this essay that appeared in *La Nouvelle Critique*, no. 3 1957 pp. 85–96.

[11] Due to the destruction of much of the housing stock by War-time hostilities, mass rural-urban migration, and a rapid rate of demographic growth, there has been a persistent and acute housing shortage in Poland ever since the Second World War. Polish factories have therefore continued, as they have done in varying degrees since as far back as the Polish industrial revolution in the second half of the nineteenth century to play an important part in housing their workers.

[12] With the exception of the Solidarity period in 1980–81, Poland in post-War years has had a system of industrial trades unionism, i.e., trades unions organised along industrial rather than craft lines, so that in each factory there would usually be only one union. At the time when Kalecki was writing, there were just under five million members of trades

unions, organised into 20 unions, whose members constituted just over 70% of the employed labour force. Together with other workers' organisations, they provided the pretext for eliminating workers' councils in 1958, when directly elected workers' representatives were incorporated with nominees of party, youth and trades union organisations into Workers' Control Conferences (Konferencje samorządu robotniczego), thereby 'safeguarding the unity of the working class'.

4 The Vertically Integrated Firm as an Element in the New Economic Model

1 The central boards (Centralne Zarządy, or, colloquially, Centrale) were organisations grouping together state enterprises by industry. The central board for each industry was answerable to the ministry dealing with its activities, and was the channel through which ministerial instructions were passed down to the enterprises. However, it had a separate accounting identity. The central boards in Poland had their powers over enterprises limited in 1956, and in 1964, they were replaced by Industrial associations that were supposed to be representative of enterprises. See J.M Montias, *Central Planning in Poland,* Yale University Press, New Haven 1962, pp. 79–81.

2 Premia (the plural of premium) are workers' bonuses and management incentive payments.

5 Outline of a New System of Incentives and Directives

1 Factory prices is the term used widely in Eastern Europe for the price obtained by a factory for its output. The factory price is equal to the retail price minus the retail (and where applicable also the wholesale) margin and the turnover, or sales, tax. In the aggregate, it is broadly equivalent to factor cost.

2 Factory funds were originaly set up in nationalised factories in Poland in 1949. A, generally small, proportion of profits is paid into the fund, and the sums accumulated therein are used for the construction of social and cultural facilities and housing for the workforce, as well as for paying bonuses to individual workers. See *Mały Słownik Ekonomiczny,* Warszawa, Państwowe Wydawnictwo Gospodarcze 1959 pp. 223–5.

3 Kalecki is here assuming a variable percentage profit mark-up, that is determined by the price set by the authorities, and the costs of the enterprise. If profits are equal to the price minus the costs of production, then the percentage profit margin will equal one minus the percentage of costs in the price.

8 On the Basic Principles of Long-term Planning

1 Partly due to good luck, favourable trade and international circumstances, and the completion of many industrial projects started at the beginning of the 1950s, that decade ended with good progress being made in economic and consumption growth. This seems to have induced a mood of optimism among the economic planners, who adopted an ambitious five-year plan for 1961–5. By 1962, this was already being revised in the light of over-investment and raw materials shortages in the economy, and payments problems in external trade. See M. Kalecki, 'Podstawowe zagadnienia planu pięcioletniego', *Gospodarka Planowa,* no. 1–2 1959 and United Nations, *Economic Survey of Europe in 1962,* Geneva 1963, chapter 1.

2 Non-productive investment, in the Material Product System of national accounting used in Eastern Europe, refers to expenditure on fixed capital in housing, public and social services, health and education. Cf. M. Kalecki, *Selected Essays on the Economic Growth of the Socialist and the Mixed Economy,* Cambridge University Press 1972, p. 3.

3 See 'Zagadnienie optymalnej struktury spożycia', *Gospodarka Planowa,* no. 7 1963 pp. 3–7.

Index